Light-Headed

A Soul-Splinter Experiences Light

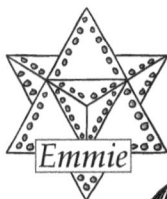

Emmie

Linda Varsell Smith

Thanks:

Maureen Frank, The Mandala Lady
for preparing the manuscript for printing,
the artwork and illustrations.
www.TheMandalaLady.com

My poetry friends and family
for their support.

ISBN: 978-0-9888554-4-1

Rainbow Communications
471 NW Hemlock Ave.
Corvallis, OR 97330

varsell4@comcast.net

Linda Varsell Smith is a teacher, poet and novelist
living in Corvallis, Oregon with husband Court
in a museum of miniatures.

CONTENTS

Light-Headed

Enlightening

Strands of Light

Patterns of Light

Daily Light

Light-Hearted

Stop and Go Light

Shades of Light

Dimmed Light

Seasonal Light

Contemplating Light

Light-Headed

Light-Headed

Perhaps the evanescent essences
of my guardian angels
encircle my head
like a gleaming halo
undetected in this dimension.

Perhaps they try to send light-beams
laser-thoughts of brilliance
into my dense, dark skull–
radiation that fails
to alter, heal, ignite insight.

Perhaps in frustration
at my thick, dull skull
and vibratory deficiency
they want to lower their halo into a noose
to strangle their unenlightened charge.

Perhaps they attempt to relay illumination
intuition and creativity
to penetrate my brain awake or asleep.
Patiently they bright-beam into my soul
hoping to transfer luminescence.

Perhaps I have been disconnected.
My halo rolls like a hula-hoop in fog.
But perhaps– out of sight, out of mind?
I would like to be a light-headed luminary
connected to a circle of numinous light.

Soulful

Soul- The lure of our becoming.   Jean Houston

There are so many definitions of soul
there must be one that fits everyone.
Soul food, soul music, soul mates,
soul engendering ethnic pride,
deep feelings, our intrinsic nature,
vital part that animates lives
and may follow the transition of death
to be reincarnated again somewhere, perhaps
in myriad forms throughout the multiverse.

Right now I am choosing
"the lure of our becoming".
It leaves openings and expansion.
As understanding and discoveries expand
soul entices me to grow,
to become more what I can be.
I don't want to grow a soul patch
but a batch of innovative insights
unfettered by limiting definitions.

Time

Time being after all, only the current of the soul in its flow. D.H. Lawrence

Perhaps time is not just about soul
and not just about human souls.

Perhaps time consists of unperceivable matter
and indecipherable matters of a cosmic nature.

Perhaps there are places without souls
or they do not mark time by celestial events.

Perhaps time exists without sentience
and our scientific definitions.

Perhaps time in space/time fabric
wrinkles and wormholes

Perhaps the passage of time in individuals
has many connotations to consider

Perhaps I should take my time,
before committing my soul to current flow.

Perhaps I will not get a time-out
toward the end of this time period.

Perhaps going with the flow
is the only option this time around.

Soul-Seeding

Souls seeded into earthly realm
with ALL at helm
blossom and grow
into the flow

Souls coded in our DNA
learn on their way,
experience
through sentience

Our souls' connected energies
with synergies
create our lives.
Souls are mid-wives.

Prayers

Help! Thanks! Wow!
Anne Lamont

There are many kinds of prayers–
many layers
seeking help
request yelp!

Others say with gratitude
up-attitude
when all goes well
heaven not hell.

Others awed by beauty gape WOW!
Seeing somehow
some things uplift
receive life's gift.

Spiritual Directors

Science is the spiritual director of our age. Sister Joan Chittister

A Catholic nun states science is the spiritual director now.
The Catholic church did not think this way in the past.
But I guess the Vatican has an observatory
and can change it's mind with different evidence.

Does wonder at the mystery of creation
and our part in it, require a spiritual director?
Can't we all think for our selves?
There are many paths to the cloud of unknowing.

Pieces of understanding can come from
physics, metaphysics, personal observations,
pundits pondering many belief systems,
math and art, nature–anywhere.

So many interpretations of a Creator
and what has been created.
So many guides speculating
and suggesting answers to unknowables.

Do humans have the capacity to comprehend
the complexity of this planet, let alone the cosmos?
We are a curious kind. We give it a try. Perhaps...
spirituality is an individual soul quest we each direct.

Non-Local Realms

If we are indeed multidimensional beings
living in diverse multidimensional spaces
with consciousness, formless or
in bodies of unimaginable compositions,
everywhere we might be prey
of light and dark forces.

Some Earthling shaman and intuitives
might communicate with these energies
in our behalf, but it is up to each of us
to choose a path of lightness or darkness
in this fleshy form while earthbound.
Our bio-bodies don't transport well in space.

The Transhumanists want to create robots,
hybrids and cyborgs to enhance the chances
humans could dwell consciously, perhaps
eternally in more multiversal circumstances.
Perhaps actions judged good or evil
will follow them wherever they go.

If everything is energy
and everything has consciousness
and this is so throughout Creation
no matter how life is expressed,
sentient beings will impact living conditions
and the starry beings they live with.

As I imagine the possibilities
of existence, I ponder the Source
or Sources that enabled it all,
if the One or Ones judge or not
and if light and dark forces
were conceived or are conceived.

Non-local realms may have other sets of rules,
more or less free will, different conceptions
of light and dark energies. In our local realm
in our fragile bodies, we have to cope
with the decisions and choices of entities
that may differ and over-ride our own.

Things are A-changing

When you change the way you look at things, the things you are looking at change. At every moment, you can either be host to God or a hostage to your ego. Wayne Dyer

When you change the way you look at things
others may view your re-vision
as you ponder what change brings
with resonance or derision.
     Ego or God are subject to interpretation
     as self-centered, dominance or veneration.

Others may view your re-vision
as contributing to the greater good
or find your shift in position
as not doing what you should.
     Do you elicit positive reaction
     or experience negative action.

As you ponder what change brings
do you hurt or heal others?
Are you follower or leader with leanings
to treat others kindly as sisters and brothers.
     In the name of God do you prey
     or uplift when you pray?

With resonance or derision
what can living beings expect?
What is your guiding vision?
What tenets do you accept or reject?
     What changes should be made
     and use your power to persuade?

Ego or God are subject to interpretation.
Extremists' faith subjects non-believers
to conformity, violence and destruction.
Do they host ego hostage or host God-retriever?
     Send light-workers for peace, my plea
     so everyone can be equal and free.

As self-centered, dominance or undo veneration
rule over justice and reason
good-hearted folks in each generation
look for a change more "pleasin"
     to host light and happiness for all
     before hostages cause our downfall.

I AM....

I Am happiness. I Am health. I Am love.   Wayne Dyer

I am happiness if I shift negative paradigm.
I am health if my mind believes it so.
I am love if I banish fear more of the time
I am creative when I express what I know.
I am courageous when act with kindness and compassion
I am connected to ALL-- never out of fashion.

I am health if my mind believes it so
My mind can make me sick or make me well.
Cures come in many ways- some from long ago.
Some cures seem miracles, as far as I can tell.
I have a better chance of healing
if my thoughts can calm from reeling.

I am love if I banish fear more of the time,
remain open to diversity of belief.
Some love appears ordinary, some sublime.
Love is not hurtful or needing relief.
I'm harmonic, committed and caring
when it's love I'm sharing.

I am creative when I express what I know
as I explore, even when not knowing for sure,
I learn, persevere and play as I go.
Expressing discoveries is creativity's lure.
When words, images, movement align,
I get a glimpse of cosmic design.

I am courageous when acting with kindness and compassion,
when I face challenges, make a difference,
move forward against limitation without distraction,
find inner strength through intuitive inference.
In a world when so many misbehave,
remember the goodness we could save.

I am connected to ALL-- never out of fashion
an energetic soul-splinter, part of the cosmos,
sentient to perform this life's mission,
consciously trying to get some meaning across.
If I could follow this mantra's intent
perhaps I could achieve why I was sent.

Our Privilege and Adventure

My predominant feeling is one of gratitude. I have loved and been loved; I have been given much and I have given something in return; I have read and traveled and thought and written...Above all I have been a sentient being, a thinking animal, on this beautiful planet, and that in itself has been an enormous privilege and adventure.   Oliver Sacks

To experience our lives with gratitude
to have loved and freely shared
to read and travel with positive attitude
to think and write well-prepared
to be a thoughtful sentient being
to explore the beauty we're seeing.

To have loved and freely shared
whatever life gifted you
acknowledges you have cared
and your living lifted you.
Sometimes when we are alone and lean
it is hard to release pain and glean.

To read and travel with positive attitude
can be difficult in certain places.
Witnessing violence and ineptitude
not even time erases,
leaves leftovers of hurt and fear
and a toxic atmosphere.

To think and write well-prepared
requires you to take action
against conditions even if scared,
to express our reaction
to global issues and events--
that activism sometimes prevents.

To be a thoughtful sentient being
requires responsibility, compassion
to work creatively for the well-being
of all life with committed passion.
Gaia has billions of beings to support
and ailing from most recent report.

To explores the beauty we're's seeing
we need to love and respect it.
Planetary stewardship is freeing.
When a problem occurs correct it.
We are in this situation together
until we release our earthly tether.

The Swing

Up in the air I go flying again/up in the air and down. "The Swing"
Robert Louis Stevenson

A young girl grabs the ropes of her swing
dangling from a sturdy branch
of a giant, verdant tree.
She pumps forward
and back
pushing higher and higher

The ropes entwine,
twist, coil, screw
as she twirls beneath.
They unravel,
let go
straighten out
she swings
higher and higher

As a grandmother I push
grandchildren on swings
until they can pump themselves.
I did the same for my children.
Now I see all my life lines
reaching higher and higher

All my life, I pull on my ropes
swing like a pendulum--
yin and yang,
getting entangled in dualities
trying to center
until I can stop swinging between
opposites or to the outer edges,
find a compatible arc,
range away from extremes,
balanced,
dreaming and anticipating,
higher and higher

Stay in the Company of Rainbows

Stay in the company of rainbows,
spiral the spectrum around your heart and vision,
sprinkle stardust on the striped light
to out-twinkle the stars.

Stay in the company of rainbows
so color merges
so color doubles and multiples
of abundance are possible.

Stay in the company of rainbows
as bridges to other dimensions,
as arches of connection.
The sky-smile hovers with light-changes.

Stay with the company of rainbows
high-humping toward heaven,
two ends touching for grounding,
a wide sturdy stance to view the universe.

Sky People, Star Beings

Invisible to me, aerial essences
contact some Earthlings
throughout time and space.

Generators of creativity,
promoters of healing,
surreal, fanciful protectors glow.

In petroglyphs and art
from ancient times
otherworldly beings stare.

In mythical stories
telling old truths
echoes reach me.

So light and airy
they appeal
to my heaviness.

Mysterious, luminous--
light up our world
before our sparkle darkles.

Things I Wish I knew

Angels' role in ALL and how angels work with people fits in.

Brain's capacity and what parts we are not using.

Cosmos' vastness and civilizations. Creative methods to know.

Destiny of our world and other unknown worlds

Energy in all its diverse expressions.

Foreign languages I do not yet understand

God in its myriad manifestations   Are guides and guardians with us?

Hybrids with alien abductions. How hope can bring change.

Inventive ways to create poems

Junk mail and why we waste paper with it. Judging its utility.

Knowledge which sets us free not confines us.

Light in or on anything

Mysteries of comic connections in mulitverses

Nuances in relationships and creativity

Openness in how we resonate with the world

Peace is elusive between humans, the environment and in mind

Questions we ask and get no answers

Radiance inside and outside of us

Science- it's the math, the formulas, the concepts I need broken down clearly

Theories- why are they so changeable and don't work for explaining things.

Understanding the complexity of ALL. Our universe is such an ort in ALL.

Violence why is it necessary on this planet and judging good and evil into conflict

Water–discovering its many uses and ways to sustain it.

Xylophones and other instruments I cannot play.

Yearning for a harmonious world when we can't seem to achieve it.

Zero. Nothing is hard to grasp in most contexts.

Amen

Organized religion is a mindless grasp of life...the religions of the world are pernicious. They're economic and political movements–if God existed they would have no particular special line to him. They're just political and social corporations. And they've been responsible for so much misery and slaughter over the years. They have such an abysmal record. They run on defrauding the public. You see all these people in their fancy costumes laying down rules as to what you can do and what you can't do and telling you it's come from God. It's so silly and people are so terrified of the situation they're in that they buy into anything. Woody Allen

Amen. Ah men. A-men B-men C-men
D-men E-men F-men GEE- men...
Men must wield the power over others.
throughout history. The other gender
is female, woman----woe man.
Allen and God both are referred to as him.

The situation is the dark night of the soul
we all confront and determine
if life is meaningless. We know we will die.
How we cope may be religious,
spiritual or secular.
Some unable to cope–opt out.

We all make our choices
and seek a rainbow
in the cloud of unknowing--
a connection that grounds the cosmos.
I'll strive for light and service,
equality, justice and love,   Ah- ALL.

Search for Certainty

How can we trust certainty in a world of change?
Are some truths actually impermeable
from outside influences?
As mind-scapes and landscapes shift
it depends where you are
      where you stand
          how stable the ground
              for you to take a stance.

Upheavals, violence, chaos
challenge our equilibrium.
We long for lightness
want to enlighten darkness.
But perceptions differ what is preferred.
      Some sustain misplaced faith
          and destructive dogma.

In the dark cosmos, light can be fire.
Not all light is conductive to biological beings.
How can we tell what we should believe
    to abide by?
        Our rules?   Other's rules?

I have preferences
what I want to be true
but that does not make it so.
    Faulty equipment my excuse?
        Genetic mutation did not give me
          the "God" gene
or the intelligence to figure out
the cosmic puzzle of which Earth
is just a minuscule piece.

I am sure of nothing
but lean toward light.

Paths Not Taken ...Yet

Every time you are tempted to react in the same old way, ask if you want to be a prisoner of the past or pioneer of the future.   Deepak Chopra

Since I am not a savant of the past
      or a predictor of the future,
      in whatever present of Now
      I am experiencing,
         I can only hope
I am not caged but open
      to new, creative ideas,
         expansive not barred.

If we create our own reality,
      can we break boundaries
         so we can explore
            wherever our curiosity leads?

Theoretically we have free will
      have choices and do not have to repeat
      choices that did not work for the betterment of All.

Circumstances do arise that clip our wings
      but is this part of our life chart
      and are there really any accidents?

I am elderly and want to draw on some old ways of wisdom,
      but I do not want to react in the same old way
      if it is not opening new paths of possibilities.

Solitary Journeys

Anything we fully do is an alone journey. Natalie Goldberg

We can create our lives with input
for decisions, choices, connections.
We can sieve what we conceive but
we journey our lives with selections
from the cosmos and the Earth
to discover our intrinsic worth.

For decisions, choices, connections
we rely on our positions and senses.
From experimental detections
we suffer for the consequences.
We face conditions where we're unable
to find ways to make chaos stable.

We can sieve what we conceive but
in dark places we need light
to break out of a habitual rut.
We need to break free of our plight.
But plunged into fear or depression
we seek release from repression.

We journey our lives with selections–
some voluntary and some appear not.
Later in puzzled recollections
we want to revise the plot,
for we know the choice is really ours
how we fulfill our designated hours.

From the cosmos and Earth
we seek answers to our whys.
Search space or ground to unearth
the ways to inform our tries.
If we look outward to learn
we find inward what we yearn.

To discover our intrinsic worth
we sometimes win and often fail.
Somehow most find a berth
to launch from and prevail.
We create our life's journey alone,
until we claim our destiny our own.

Go Be Light

Go be Light. Don't stand for anything wrong. Don't stand for evil. Break it up. Go break it up Go be light! Go be strong! Don't put up with anything dark. Go bring light! Go be light. Stand for light.   Dolores Cannon

Stand up for light.
Break up evil and wrong.
Act on what feels right.
Go bring light! Be strong!
      But on Earth it's hard to be patient
      to remain open and resilient.

Break up evil and wrong.
Life can overwhelm the staunchest soul.
Difficult times tend to prolong
and when broken, it's hard to get whole.
      Will we proceed like Sisyphus
      or is there a different plan for us?

Act on what feels right
with strong light in Darth Vader dark.
Light-beings shine bright
being light wherever we embark.
      Break it up. Show up. Speak up.
      Step in to fill an empty cup.

Go bring light! Be strong!
Bravely do what needs to be done.
Our light-tasks are lifelong–
for everyone. We're all one.
      Try to do the tough stuff.
      Believe you're good enough.

But on Earth it's hard to be patient
when all seems beyond one's control.
Can we meditate and remain silent?
Should we be out on light patrol?
      Can we bring a stellar glow
      so what's above is below?

To remain open and resilient,
to sustain your inner glow
helps you to achieve your intent
no matter where you choose to go.
      Ride Miley Cyrus' wrecking ball.
      Anchor the light. Stand tall.

Enlightening

Cosmic Consanguinity

Who writes the script for our being
on this planet during this time?
What mysteries are we not seeing
in the mundane and the sublime?
Are we directed by comic kin?
Who shares lives in this stardust bin?

On this planet during this time
what creators are in control,
whose resources do they prime?
How large a dominion do they patrol?
Our thoughts derive from somewhere.
I wish we could be more aware.

What mysteries are we not seeing?
The big questions of meaning,
from some sources decreeing
while we are not gleaning
our full cosmic purpose now.
I wish I could know somehow.

In the mundane and the sublime
clues to our essence could be revealed.
Are we just here to mime
and our true nature concealed?
Noone available to testify?
I wish I could have answers to why.

Are we directed by cosmic kin–
alien cousins, angels, spirit guides?
From what dimension are they in?
We're left to what the cosmos provides.
Free will? Seems others make our choices.
I wish harmonically All rejoices.

Who shares lives in this stardust bin?
Our thoughts derive without our senses.
Other sentience sources are within
our soul has other presences.
While we dream, and hope eternally
I wish we lived in a peaceful reality.

Seeking Internal Wormholes

The longest journey you will ever take is between your head and your heart.
Gary Zukav

Earth School's curriculum
tends to brainwash your head
to manipulate your heart.

Even the best quality of brain signals
may not ever reach the heart–
a heart too damaged to receive.

As multi-sensory perception
and mind expansion increases
will the heart expand also?

Along our journey with variously impaired equipment
emotions tug at head and heart.
Can a positive way find a direct route?

What kind of GPS can help us
find our destination
and who will travel with you?

What guide books and gurus will you select?
Pit stops can be hazardous.
Brain glitches and heartache prevalent.

Traffic signals and signs,
other travelers confronted.
Bi-ways and highways congested.

Your head concusses with impacts--
physical and mental– impairs thought,
confuses ideas and direction.

The journey from head to heart
might not always be attempted. Sometimes
we chose to dwell in each terminal a while.

Some head concepts are not relevant
to an unreceptive heart,
delaying any transmission.

Surface maps do not always get us
to our destination or find hidden treasure.
We might fly, derail, freewheel.

Some of our thoughts might not be
intended for heart reception.
It is best they remain detached.

Some of our heart's passions, not sieved by thought
never consult the head for wisdom
and randomly splat the path.

A mentally ill mother tosses autistic son London
off of a bridge, a dementia patient
is not able to know a way around.

The long journey between head and heart
may not be a goal or possible for some.
Our purposes might not require such contact.

All I think is not compatible with my highest heart
or mind. This reality I construct
does not support all I perceive.

The heart and head contain contradictions.
When they meld, I can only hope
they bridge love and tunnel light.

Each being quests with individual intent,
deals with the equipment given
and insights acquired en route.

Wormholes connect instantaneously
one reality to another.   Inside us
we take a circuitous route........slowly.

Questioning Patience

Be patient toward all that is unsolved in your heart and try to love the questions themselves. Live the questions now. Perhaps you will gradually, without noticing, live along some distant day into the answer. Rainier Maria Rilke

There is that word *patient* again.
I postponed patience to my next incarnation.

My bruised heart is anxious for befuddled beloveds
and all the unsolved violence in the world.

I do love to question existence, but forbearance
for living without many answers frustrates me.

I am a persevering optimist protesting wars,
chaos, polluted water, air and land.

Intolerant with misguided authority, greed,
injustice, inequality and irresponsibility,

impatient with lack of consistent action
to address Earth's sustainability issues.

Perhaps we can be too patient, too passive,
too accepting of limitations.

Some distant day I expect few answers,
but perpetual questions. I will notice.

I thrive on questions, curiosity,
creativity— patience not so much.

In this world of yin and yang, can I balance,
find a middle way from extremes?

My decision to release patience frees me
to continue to probe and act.

I'll probably end up a patient in a mental ward
because I can't accept patiently this delusional reality.

Perusing the Web

Find your way. Diana Nyad

When your life chart gets erased
to a blank slate at birth,
you might be perplexed
how to find your way
in this new experience--
but you are never alone.
You are always connected to All
and guides are by your side.

Miracles and mysteries await
as we explore this gift of existence.
We need to remember gratitude
for this opportunity to live
even when the reality we created
does not jive with our hopes.
Can we find a way to plug in
to cosmic life energy
and exercise free will
for positive choices?

Can we break from the cocoon
to become a butterfly and fly?
Will we probe for things
unseen on the surface,
dig in for courage to try again?
The quality of light differs
every moment. Plants dance
toward the light, lust for bees
to keep the web of life alive.
Nature's beauty can open our hearts
to nurture and protect what we love.

We are responsible for the energy we emit.
We can focus on the higher good for all creation.
Consciousness is in everything.
We are all connected.
Energize the cosmic web.
What matters is what you do now.
What you planned on the Other Side
might not have manifested exactly
as you planned this lifetime, but
find a way to make the best connections.

BLAH

BLAH: Be Loving And Helpful   Doreen Virtue

Feeling lower case blah after watching
Oprah's Super Soul Sunday
with Deepak Chopra, Eckhart Tolle
and three young spiritual leaders'
inspiring words about their clear
direct lines to the Divine.
I iced my knees, as I listened
feeling my connection to All needed work,
then ordered Omega3 vitamins and napped.

I watched a video of Doreen Virtue
on how to do a three card reading
picking three cards after praying over them
to help someone or yourself answer questions.
Think about it --what you are saying
as a telephone to heaven.
The prayer: to let you be of service,
and provide value and meaning.

I had various cards from my New Age stage
but somehow I misplaced them.
So I decided to pick three runes.
Past, present and future.
Past was a reversed Ehwaz
the rune of transit, transition and movement.
It indicates a sense of gradual development.
But mine was reversed indicating movement
appears blocked. I had to realize
not all opportunities are appropriate.
I feel at a loss, unclear about the need to act,
what is timely to my nature and remember:
What is yours will come to you.

For the present I picked upside down Laguz
which relates to flow, a time for revaluing,
reorganizing and realigning, to study
spiritual matters in readiness for self-transformation.
It relates to awakening intuitive and lunar side
toward union and merging. But I picked reversed
a counsel against overreach and excessive striving,
a failure to draw on wisdom of instinct, leaving
me out of balance and languishing intuitively.
I need to go within to honor my receptive side.

For the future there is no reverse for Jera,
a rune of beneficial outcomes and harvest
to any endeavor you are committed to-- but
no quick results can be expected.
A span of time is usually involved- one year.
I have prepared the ground, planted the seed,
now must cultivate with care. For those whose labor
has a long season, a long coming to term,
Jera offers encouragement to succeed.
The outcome is in keeping of Providence,
so keep persevering. Be patient for
the recognition of your own process leads
to the harvest of the self, in its season.

After decades of studying physics, metaphysics,
spirituality, the arts and poetry, teaching creative writing
to others so they can express their experiences,
pondering the cosmos and Earth's past–
I set the goal on my 75th birthday
I would complete two books of poetry
before I turned 76. I have been told
they will be my last two of three books,
so I am committed
to completing them despite physical
and emotional challenges.
The mind makes one sick and can make one heal.
I am trying several approaches
for this to help me achieve what
I need to know, to do what I want to do.

Doreen Virtue shouts BLAH after a successful reading.
An epigram by Dr. Samuel Johnson to Book of Runes:
To lend courage to virtue and ardor to truth.
I strive to go from blah to BLAH
whatever card or rune I'm dealt.

Letting Go

The fact is, you already know how to find yourself, you have just gotten distracted and disoriented. Once refocused, you will realize that you not only have the ability to find yourself, you have the ability to free yourself.
Michael Singer

Mind makes body sick or makes well
I've many parts to try to heal.
I'm not succeeding I can tell.
I need lessons how I should feel.

First they ask you just who are you?
The flow of emotions come and go.
You is one who'll consciously know.
Then they suggest what you should do.
Not a basket case when you're through.
We must train our neurotic mind.
You're an experiencer. You'll find
 intuitive sense to express
 awareness, consciousness.
Getting there? I'm still in a bind.

Commit to your inner freedom
release habitual mind so
from witness seat your life can flow,
but I still face a conundrum,
just what am I now fleeing from?
Spiritual practices can
help you gain knowledge to expand.
Distance yourself from your psyche.
You can be free, swoosh like Nike.
Not that easy I understand.

You are behind things just watching.
From seat of self you are aware
a world of senses come from there.
Just what is it I'm not catching,
my reality not matching?
Somehow this is still too abstract
I'm conscious receiver is a fact.
Thinking the thought, I'm lucid--
a tad difficult like Euclid
when it's pain you have to extract.

Makes sense theoretically
World is something you are watching.
experiences you're swatching.
But letting go is hard for me.
I am not sure I can be free.
Who am I is the question?
The answer is suggestion.
Truth, our minds expend energy
Can I hope for some synergy,
relax, open, clear congestion?

You watch as mind does the thinking.
Let go of the chaos inside.
Be aware, release crazy side.
I don't feel my issues shrinking.

Be Happy

Committing yourself to unconditional happiness will teach you every single thing there is to learn about yourself, others and about the nature of life. You will learn all about your mind, your heart and your will...Every time a part of you begins to get you unhappy, let it go. Michael Singer

The highest spiritual path is life itself.
Knowing how to live is liberating.

Do you choose to live life happily?
You can decide and become enlightened.
Unconditional happiness is highest technique there is.

You just choose to be happy and mean it.
This is a spiritual path to Awakening.

Your life's purpose is to enjoy and learn from experiences.
Can you be happy no matter what happens?

Do you want to enjoy your life?
The highest spiritual path is life itself.

You just choose to be happy and mean it.
Between life and death, why not be happy?
Open your heart. Your spirit will be free.

You win the game if you stay happy.
Play the game to be happy no matter what happens.

Be Happy...When You Can.

You have limited time left in your life, and what's not really reasonable is to not enjoy life...you're always aware enough not to allow your heart to close. You remain open by simply letting go and releasing the tendency to close. You just relax your heart when it starts to tighten....Instead of complaining, you're just having fun with different situations that unfold. Unconditional happiness is a very high path and a very high technique because it solves everything.
Michael Singer

My heart does not close but pours pain
as I read of a 12-year-old girl, raped
by an Islamic State fighter. He would gain
Allah's praise. But when she escaped
she told the harrowing tale,
when her faith did not prevail.

As I read of a 12-year-old girl. raped
because she was not of his belief,
he book-ended rape with prayer, agaped,
tied and gagged her, provided no relief,
told her it was not a sin but Ibadah's will
to submit to Allah, obedience to instill

by an Islamic State fighter. He would gain
closer to God by this godless act.
Islamic State enslaved Yazidi women to rape again.
Over 5,270 Yazidis in one year abducted in fact.
Warehoused women inspected and marketed.
Repressed recruits were lured and targeted.

Allah's praise? But when she escaped,
she made international news.
Shocked, many recoiled and gaped,
appalled by traditional taboos
enshrined in core tenets of the group,
outside humanity's compassion loop.

She told the harrowing tale
identified only by her first name.
God's protection did fail.
Rape is associated with shame.
She was the victim of the misguided,
left in sorrow after attention subsided.

When her faith did not prevail--
nor would mine in that situation--
what happiness, fun could she avail
amid a code of devastation?
So be happy when you can,
you could be captured by another's plan.

Mantra for the New Year

Flip each day into a new game of unimagined Possibility
Beguile us from old patterns. Charm us into Change.
She-Who-Jests, crack us up. Crack us open.
HA! O Queen of Play   Bethroot Gwynn*

Flip each day into a game of unimagined Possibility
Beguile us from old patterns, create something new.
Charm us into change, find routes for accessibility
She-Who-Jests lightens the world view.
Crack us up so we are uplifted.
Crack us open so all are gifted.

Beguile us from old patterns, create something new,
care and share with light-giving ways.
Where will our guidance come through?
Sift carefully for what stays.
When we leave ancient constructs,
build, leave behind what destructs.

Charm us into change, find routes for accessibility
Use GPS, not just maps to get where we're going.
Change can enhance your credibility.
Remember to keep our instincts glowing.
A digital age is in your hands
as our consciousness expands.

She-Who Jests lights the world view
when the planet looks dark and dim.
Try to be positive, enlighten, renew
even when our hopes look grim.
Bring promise to the Anthropocene!
Make our impact sustainably clean.

Crack us up so we are uplifted.
From our roots sprout wings.
Maybe our consciousness shifted?
Excitement for what the future brings?
Strive for activities we can enjoy
and discoveries we can employ.

Crack us open so all are gifted
by our presence and life's meaning,
re-steer our course when we've drifted,
create from messages we're gleaning
a climate changed world to benefit all
as we listen for destiny's call.

Knock Knock

What uninvited, unexpected visitor
knocks at my door?
Proselytizer or peddler
what are you trying to sell me?
Pamphlets or personal persuasion
to convert me to your concepts
or purchase your products?

Whether it is from ardent religious zeal
or means of survival, sellers intrude
into my choices in life and privacy.

This time it is two young men
my grandsons' age with elder badges.
They have come before,
spied my angel collection through door-glass
and considered me an easy target.
Some elders even asked to photograph
my angels.   I did not ask for their advice
before I politely ushered them out.

Should I bother to open the door
or just nod no through the glass?
Need I explain why I don't go to church,
prostrate before their gods or gurus,
worship their interpretations
of the creator of the universe
and cosmic emissaries,
or share meanings of this planetary existence?

I have listened to their point of view before,
have heard and read about their professions
of love, delivered with fear

Faith does not need the answers to the Big Questions
verified by science, philosophy or any approach.
Spirituality is an individual quest.
We can decide ourselves,
if open-minded and not brainwashed.
I have accepted the "cloud of unknowing".

I think I'll light the lamp post,
        to lead them
                away.

Seeking Cosmic Directions

Once there were many gods,
then one god
and for some no god.
So many choices
for cosmic directions.

Each religion has their chosen
messenger from a chosen god
with various degrees of divinity.
Culture values dictate
most messengers be male.

Each religion has rituals,
rules of conduct,
ways to pay homage
as some gods and messengers
elicit worship and prayers.

Each religion protects turf.
Wars and inquisitions
keep faithful in line,
despite most preach
similar values.

Spirituality outside organized religion
can also promote a personal
relationship with the divine
or find bearings without
a godly component or science.

The quest is how can we behave
with kindness, love and compassion
and find meaning to our existence
and possible after-life
with tolerance, commitment, peace.

Conflicting Belief

Contemplate this, and let go of the idea of a judgmental God. You have a loving God. In truth, you have love itself for a God. And love cannot do other than love. Your God is in ecstasy and there is nothing you can do about it.
Michael Singer

People around the world interpret
what is the nature of God
and what connection do we have
to the Divine—or a Cosmic Plan.

Some say God is without judgment
just in ecstasy over creation
filled with love, compassion, joy
eternal conscious bliss.

Some religions have certain rules
how one must believe and behave
to worship their way. If you did have a choice
and varied, you are punished.

Wars, inquisitions, torture result
when beliefs presume dominance
and feel it is God's will to crush
the will of a non-believer.

If we are part of All and God
expects us to experience lives
all over the cosmos and bring back
knowledge for cosmic libraries–why?

If Divine Consciousness is omniscient,
omnipresent and omnipotent–a force
that is aware of all things at all times
equally–universally conscious–why us?

Ibadah states the reason for all existence
is for all people to submit to Allah with love,
obedience, submission and devotion.
They consider rape, violence and slavery God's will.

Bible-thumpers justified slavery, inquisitions
by their holy book. Male hierarchies
East and West pronounced God's will,
used a male pronoun, dominated women.

To get transcendence and higher vibrations
closer to God involves following
a spiritual path speculated on by others-
the Tao or a path some seekers suggested.

At the same time we have free will
if not stiffled by someone else's rules.
If God does not judge, we get stuck
doing so when it causes suffering.

What if our planet is under
some Galactic Federation-
the spoils of a good and evil battle.
Maybe dark beings won and light flickers here.

Perhaps negativity slipped in
during upheavals and disruptions
to the divine plan for Earth.
Are we supposed to worship a conqueror?

It is wonderful to believe in a warm-fuzzy God,
erasing karmic and chronic suffering,
so we can join our cosmic cousins,
standing tall not on our knees.

The nature of The Source,
the energy experiments of Creation,
are still a source of wonder and puzzlement,
as I untether my soul on my cosmic quest.

There may be glitches in God's plan.
We may not have the capacity to correct errors.
If God is indeed perfect–the product is not.
We are left to muddle through seeking love, light.

Scriptures predict a dire ending
for not doing God's will–but God is not a judge?
Who will steward the planet's creatures
and struggling life forms surrounding us?

I'm supposed to let go and be happy
but I am responsible for beyond me.
Alas, my soul must remain tethered to love,
commitments, service while on Earth.

Stardusters Unite

We are all in this together
despite our superficial skin,
all hold the silver cord tether,
from stardust we begin.
> We dwell on our difference.
> Act on our preference.

Despite our superficial skin
and cultural costume,
we are alike deep within
and try our best, I presume.
> Some dark beings bring wrath
> when lead off their lighter path.

All hold the silver cord tether
until it's severed and released.
Then there is no question whether
we're still living or deceased.
> Until we're no longer at the helm,
> we create our lives in this realm.

From stardust we begin,
manifest earthly creatures,
just like cosmic kin
with individual features.
> If we could be compassionate and kind
> a more peaceful existence we'd find.

We dwell on our difference
we find in others, eliciting fear.
Look for a love reference
and ways to keep vision clear.
> Until more truth is spoken,
> we'll remain heart-broken.

Act on our preference
for caring and connection.
Use our gift of sentience
to make a light-bearing selection.
> Keep up a high-five vibe
> with others of the stardust tribe.

Strands of Light

Imprinting

Words are the fingerprints of the soul. Daniel Day-Lewis

Unfold the fist of spirit.
Unknuckle the hands from prayer.
Finger-mark words on the page–
inklings of the cloud of unknowing.

Imprint ideas from your meandering mind
to record your soul's journey.
Words are one way to finger the essence
of what remains intangible.

Lighting the Muse

Ignite a spark in my mind.
Turn on a lightbulb moment.
What illumination will I find.?
Will I be agitated or content?
I hope I can be resilient
even when I can't be brilliant.

Turn on a lightbulb moment.
Reveal shadows on a wall.
Clarify a dimmed comment.
Make me ready for any call.
Keep those sluggish neurons twitching
with something bright and bewitching.

What illumination will I find
in my brain's murky parts.
What should be left behind
or rush toward the ramparts?
What should I draw near?
What ideas can appear?

Will I be agitated or content
to express what's uncovered?
Is it part of life's experiment?
Will I face what I discovered?
Or will I be diminished by age
consumed by apathy or rage?

I hope I can be resilient
and words are the last to go.
Can I cling to being sentient
and will I even know?
Please keep a creative connection
as my mind makes a selection.

Even when I can't be brilliant
I appreciate word-play.
Words are luminescent
and brighten each day.
So when my wits darkle,
let some remnants sparkle.

Left-Handed

I'm
left
handed.
I lean left,
favor left viewpoints-
liberal with equality.

I'm
left
behind
and left out
with some tech progress–
left in the lurch without tutor.

I'm
left
to muse
on right thing
to do and create.
This lefty could be left alone.

Blocked Today

Today is a cloudy gray day--
a day when my thoughts skitter
amidst angst for loved ones
suffering illness and distance.

This poem needs a form
to pull thoughts together
to give me a spine
to deal with
to flow into lines
the release of anxiety
I need to express.

Usually words press into a page
with my tight hand.
But today I peck at computer keys
with both hands, peeking at the keys,
unable to settle my restless fingers.
Thoughts sputter onto the screen.
I find words but they do not say
what I am thinking.

This is a fast, first draft
which will not see a second draft
at least not today.

Browsing Through My Word-hoard

Trying to catch right words
to capture my thoughts.
I can't lasso my word-hoard
no corralling word-herds.

Sounds and letters are particles
invisible mini-bytes un-wrought
uncontrollable sparticles
un-composed lost articles.

Un-glommed images
floating not landing
not trapped by pages
released from word-cages.

Nothing comes together
Nothing understanding
my need to word-tether
in turbulent word-weather.

Marking Poems

In books I prefer
no markings on the page.
Other's comments can be written
upon separate paper.
I want to imprint my mind
with my own responses
to the writer's intentions.
Go-betweens remarks
should remain private
and not divert my attention.

When creating my own poems-
scribbling, crossing out
ink-smudged fingers
sweaty palms–
my marks leak thoughts
on my paper to get typed
on my computer
for further revision
of what I thought or
what I wanted to share.
Perhaps the poems will be in a book
and someone will write
directly on the poem.
Maybe I would want to see it.

Be True to Form

Writing poetry makes imagination real
Writer's block becomes an alibi
thwarts the joy of creation
Seek to be a soul freed
so you can form your agenda

Poetry and Hums

"But it isn"t easy," said Pooh, "Because Poetry and Hums aren't things which you get, they're things which get you. And all you can do is go where they find you." The House at Pooh Corner

It's all the way you hum--
not always drone or humdrum,
you can hum with action
and sing without opening lips.

Poetry hums on the page,
hums words to linger in the mind.
Hum, like a thoughtful pause.
Hum, in annoyance.

Hums and poetry resonate
Some are humdingers.
I like hum in humor
and not humbug.

Poetry can be musical,
hum in our heart
without opening our mouth--
felt humongously.

Like a hummingbird seeks nectar,
humans find poetry.
Hummers of the world
hum with delight!

Playing with Poems

The best poetry has its roots in the subconscious to a great degree. Youth,
naivete, reliance on instinct more than learning and method, a sense of freedom
and play, even trust in randomness, is necessary to the making of a poem.
                    May Swenson

Dipping into the cosmic consciousness
          tripping through the Akashic records,
dreaming images, exploring multi-dimensionality,
          stimulating the senses when fully awake,
               increases the odds I will find the inklings of a poem
                    delightfully playing with my aging mind to page.

Downloading the subconscious
          from the cosmic consciousness
produces the images and words to play into a poem.
          Traveling through dimensions,
perhaps glints of simultaneous lives
          informs our Earthly sentience.

I dally with forms- love the poem puzzles.
          I research fascinations to share discoveries.
I devour new words, plunk them into poems
          and into cooperative Scrabble games
          sprawling on board and tablecloth
               into new patterns to ponder--
                    unexpected connections to contemplate.

Poems try to line up chaos,
          greet randomness as a challenge
               and find serendipitous resonance.
Poems are free to be.
          I am still naive to believe
          poetry is the most magical, compelling expression
               of our perplexing earthly experience.

Oregon Poetry Collection
February 2013   Oregon State Library, Salem

Books of Oregon poets are found
on the second floor-- the northern end.
The collection is in a closed off area
entered by an open doorway.
The high ceiling is ornate
with tall rectangular paneled walls.
The collection is on your right as you enter
the reference room.

Photos of the Oregon Poet Laureates line the top shelves:
Edwin Markham, Ben Hur Lampman, Ethel Romig Fuller,
William Stafford, Lawson Inada, Paulann Petersen.
Most have a book of theirs beside the photo.
Around 1581 books on the shelves.
With duplicates for circulation 3017.
White spine label on the upright bindings.
Other shelves hold magazines and newspapers.

Two rows of shelves beneath the Laureates
six book cases long for dead and living poets.
Beneath a window is a desk from the First
Oregon Legislative Assembly and an old,
historic chair which we must not sit on.

There are eight mustard colored comfy chairs
with four end tables between them.
Dangling lights, perhaps bronze look golden.
The rug has diamonds of green and gold-ish.
I can check on the books I donated
and the donations of others.
I know I need to cull more books from my collection
to give to this library so the poetry books
can be read and have a secure home.

Still many empty shelves for more poetry book donations.
More books need to get into circulation.
After poetry books have been read and enjoyed,
we can share them to preserve Oregon's poetic legacy.

Addendum 2015: The State Library budget was curtailed. The
collection is now housed at the University of Oregon in Eugene.

Air Bearing - Air Trooping

Tinted owl perches on Underwood typewriter
imprinted on aged dictionary page–
a gift from son made my day brighter.

A collaged image reflects me at this stage–
a techno-turd, skills obsolete
imprinted on aged dictionary page.

Now framed, the picture is complete.
It's symbolism is pretty clear–
a techno-turd, skills obsolete.

Heading words: air bearing to air trooping appear.
Word-smithing, winging-it, I airily align.
It's symbolism is pretty clear.

Owl wisdom or owl's call death's near sign?
Strong message of writer-passion shared.
Word-smithing, winging-it, I airily align.

I'm touched someone thought of me and cared.
Tinted owl perches on Underwood typewriter.
Strong message of writer-passion shared.
A gift from son made my day brighter.

Words Yell and Yelp

Even words are going somewhere urban. W.S. Merwin

As billions of people crowd into cities,
their words resonate against concrete and metal,
resound off screens, walls of glass.
Some words connect with other people
with forced closeness in containers.
Some words remain inner screams.

From rural, isolated places words yowl,
float over processed landscapes.
Even in wild places seekers' words cough
on allergans and particulates, pleading
to the universe for salvation
from melting mountaintops.

Words go urban, clustering in lighted places,
where intermittently the power goes off.
Obscured stars receive muted praise
from dimmed reflections on glass.
Text messages and calls relay instant words,
hope for a reply from somewhere.

Losing Words

After seeing the movie Still Alice
portraying a linguist losing words
due to Familial Early Onset Alzeheimer's,
I could picture the city near Auschwitz
but not remember the name of Krakow.
I was ready to get my DNA tested
even though I am too old for early onset.

So I pondered Poland and thought
I could remember Warsaw
by war saw ghetto, my most vivid
image there except parking on sidewalks.

Losing words, my joy in word play,
sharing discoveries, I think
of Stephen Hawking at some point
totally caging words inside him.

To know I am losing words and memory
until I can no longer remember,
or communicate, without words,
when memory is oblivion--
staring into space, unable
to connect, to say where I am...

Until then I will play Scrabble,
gather more words anywhere I can,
write poems to recall
memories, explore concepts,
relish and celebrate naming.

Twitterpated

In this age of concise Twitter
you can't express much when smitten:
roar as lion, soft as kitten.
Sometimes the tweet might be bitter
or an out of ballpark hitter.
Less love letters in high-tech age.
Most tweets don't even reach a page.
New ways to be twitterpated.
Still love words appreciated,
no matter how they engage.

Art

Art transforms the creator, the viewer, the performer, the listener: art transforms us all. Lisa Noble

Staring at a blank screen
blanched page, newly stretched canvas
un-molded media, rehearsal script
art is a possibility,
until the muse appears--
creators chaotic, audience fickle.

Art is chancy, changes.
Composing or watching
I want to be part of art
engaged in enlightened energy.
Space/time finds the God Particle
and we all are divine.

Siuslaw Angel

Silk on canvas painting by Denise DeKemper

Siuslaw angel lifts in blue sky
       over the edge of the sea
            drifts near evergreens and sand.

Round, beige head without facial features--
       spiral- face, a galaxy connecting to cosmos,
           without hair or halo.

No arms, but wings like fringed clouds,
       lavender gown flows like wavelets
           over bare, toe-less feet.

She is unframed, between two painted, pale- purplish bands
       I want to fly, light-headed, with this anonymous angel
           hovering over Oregon's southern shoreline.

Driving Home

Clouds gulp the moon.
Sky-sculptures morph.
Autumn hues splay the trees,
dropping leaves, waiting
to whirl in wind.

After a poetry reading,
inhaling light, I deep breathe
into the prosaic world
waiting for a breakthrough,
glimpse of moonlight.

Patterns of Light

The Dance of Love and Light

Listening to merkaba music,
I found my feet, dancing
to its cosmic beat.

Apparently Sacred Merkaba Techniques
can teach me how to join in
the cosmic dance of love and light.

One can expand the size of consciousness
in one's Light Body to a Love-Love body to experience
multiple dimensional levels simultaneously.

Imagine all the diverse light forms
that could manifest to be my partners
in mysterious, magical locales.

Here I can imagine dancing up my spine
and play chakras like a child's colorful xylophone.
But I need a different body for cosmic dancing.

Apparently, we are at one of the moments
of great leaps of understanding
like in human's Earthly past.

Merkaba is a doorway or dimensional window
into a higher level of consciousness,
a catalyst of Ascension.

Merkaba is unfolding worldwide.
Millions are part of the evolving cosmic DNA.
Once it is alive, anything is possible.

I want to dance the dance of love and light
with energies of unconditional love.
Millions activate merkaba's magnetic bursts.

Some claim most powerful governments use it.
Merkabas can be put on computer screens via satellite.
If I ever get tracked and spied on–I 'd want to be dancing.

Cosmic Dancing

Dance Shiva dance
Dance Shiva dance
Make everything brand new
Give us another chance
Jai Uttal Kirten

The cosmic dance of Shiva symbolizes the interplay of dynamic and static divine energy flow, containing the five principles of eternal energy—creation, preservation, destruction, illusion and emancipation. KP Shashidyharan

Nataraja, the dancing form of Shiva, Lord of the Dance
dances the rhythm and harmony of life
in a circle of fire, a flaming halo, the manifest universe
which encapsulates the cosmos of mass, time and space,
a cycle of annihilation and regeneration, moving
in time to Shiva's drum beat and rhythmic steps.

Four arms like bamboo stalks fling in cardinal directions.
Left foot raises triumphant over illusion and ignorance.
Right foot on huddled, ignorant demon dwarf.
Snakes of egotism slither from limbs and tresses.
The snake around his waist is kundalini,
the divine force believed to be within everything.
His knotted, matted hair loosens as he dances
creating cosmic chaos, knocking off course
or demolishing heavenly bodies.
Shiva dances to destroy in order to create,
tears down to build again,
dances with ash on his forehead.

Shiva's cosmic dance is called Anandatandava
or Dance of Bliss symbolizing the cosmic cycle
of creation and destruction, birth and death.
Lasya is a gentle dance and Tandava
his violent, dangerous dance.
Cosmic dance is a continual dance of the whole cosmos,
the basis of all existence and all natural phenomena.

Shiva's dance portrays rhythmic play, universal movement
even of the subatomic particles.
Bronze Shiva statues dance in temples and at CERN.
The purpose of the dance is to release souls from illusion.
The place of the dance is in the sky of the mind
at the altar of the heart.
Not the center of the universe.
He dances on a lotus pedestal which represents
the creative forces of the universe.

Shiva, the symbol of universal consciousness
watches with an omniscient, enlightened third eye,
gestures to us to be fearless
as he dances to create, maintain,
destroy the universe.
Shiva's neutral gaze indicates
balance and neutrality,
inner tranquility amid outside chaos.
A skull on his head shows
conquest over death.
A moon symbol, should it fall,
means the end of the universe.
For now Shiva dances encircled by fire
often frozen in bronze.

Dancing is an art, unifies art and artist,
evokes the oneness of creation.
Cosmic dancing connects religious art,
ancient mythology and modern physics.
The energy dance of subatomic particles
is part of a pulsing process
of creation and destruction.

Will I cosmically dance alone?
I'd prefer a playful partner to lightly lead
but not to follow or to worship divine Creators.
I envision cosmic thoughts discarnate.
I tend to distrust personified deities,
embodied representatives.
Shiva holds an hourglass drum
symbolizing male-female vital energy
but he performs as male
often in heavy metal.
I prefer diaphanous, androgynous angels
with enlightening intent.

Dance angels dance
Dance angels dance
Halos glow light as you flow,
choreograph for partners to know

May I lovingly Wu Li dance
in this elegant, graceful universe
with a joyful, multiversal beat
listening for the sound of aum.

Lords A-Leaping

I danced in the morning when the world was begun
I danced in the moon and the stars and the sun.
I was called from the darkness by the song of the earth....
I joined in the singing and she gave me birth   (Traditional : Celtic)

The Lord of the Dance helps all things to grow,
leads rituals, folk dances from long, long ago,
celebrates the seasons, harvests joys,
protects from weather, all rejoice.

I danced in the morning when the world was begun
I danced in the moon and the stars and the sun
I came down from heaven and I danced on the earth
At Bethlehem I had my birth (Sydney Carter: Hymn)

The Lord of the Dance is not just Jesus,. he
dances shape and pattern for heart of reality.
Dances as Christ in other times and places
even other planets, dimensional spaces.

I danced in the morning when the world was begun
I danced in the moon and the stars and the sun
I danced Irish dance, and gave new worth.
I joined dance with singing for a rebirth (for Lord of the Dance
Musical)

The Lord of the Dance hosts a musical gig
leads dances worldwide to Irish jig.
Young Lordlings twirl with straight armed leaps
click heels so from evil goodness reaps.

I danced in the morning when the world was begun
I danced in the moon in the stars and the sun.
I danced for destruction to create the new,
might destroy the universe when I'm through.
(for Nataraja, Shiva Lord of the Dance)

The Lord of the Dance flails his four arms
sometimes enhances, sometimes harms.
Stomps on a demon and lifts left leg high,
gives annihilation and regeneration a try.

Lords of the Dance a-leaping all over the world
Lords of the Dance a-sweeping, gracefully swirled.
Lords the Dance perform for many seasons.
Lords of the Dance have their own reasons.

Dance, dance, wherever you may be
I am the Lord of the Dance said he
And I lead you all, wherever you may be
I lead you all in the dance, said he   (Sydney Carter: Hymn)

The moon in her phases and the tides and the sea
The movement of Earth, and the seasons that will be
Are rhythm for the dancing and the promise through the years–
The Dance goes on through joy and tears.   (Traditional: Celtic)

Dancing Goddesses

Around the world since ancient times
dancing goddesses dance for creation.
Goddesses invite us all to dance.,
partner for celebrations.
Dance to bond people
and communities together in rituals
Dance to music to stir your soul.
Dance to lead or cajole.

Dance to energize the earth
Dance to help Gaia breathe
Dance in gratitude for living
Dance to stomp fear
Dance to honor the dead
Dance to mourn, teach.
Dance to delight, outreach.

Dance to the rhythms of harmony
Dance for the hope of transformation
Dance for fertility in flora, fauna, families
Dance to mediate or entice feelings
Dance to empower young girls.
Dance in lines, loops and twirls.

Dance to express art and joy
to choreograph dreams
to release tension
heal illness
reduce fatigue
to free your body.
Dance is the essence and motion of life.

Dance to the beat of the cosmos
Energized stardust--
twinkle those toes
spiral like galaxies
join the multiversal dance

Dance everyone dance
Dance everyone dance
Dance to celebrate love and light
Dance to enhance rituals and delight
Dance everyone dance

Dancing with Derek

So I need to see you again and again, although I know you are not meant for me.
Kim Trainor

When I see Derek Hough dance
I am mesmerized.
I could watch him dance
with anyone and alone.
His choreography, grace,
such zestful energy–
ah–delightful.

My grandchildren tease me saying
"Grandma loves Derek".
They cannot understand it is not just him
but his dances I love.

My granddaughter says, "Derek is gay."
I tell her I don't care.
He is not meant to be my partner
in any sense.

Recently he danced "Singing in the Rain"
in the style of his idol Gene Kelly.
He received another perfect score
on Dancing with the Stars
for this charming performance.

Each show I double-vote for him,
devoted to Derek's creative genius
no matter who is his partner,
no matter the couples he competes against.
I have good taste.
He's won two Emmys for his choreography
as well as six seasons on the show.

I saw Derek dance in Radio City Music Hall
in New York Spring Spectacular. I waited
at the stage door to tell him how much
I enjoy his dancing and book.

I have a photo of me talking with him.
I saw him in Move Live On Tour with his sister Julianne
in a stop in Portland, but did not wait in line.

For me at 75 with arthritic knees
I am not meant for dance now
but all my life when I could dance or couldn't
I know dance, but not Derek
is meant for me.

January 2017 Derek Hough has the leading role in Singing in the Rain on Broadway

MOVE

How I would love to really move,
be able to feel joy of dance,
but with these bad knees– not a chance.
I dare to feel, cry, try and love.
Watching them dance in bright alcove.
I remember my dancing days
when I could move in playful ways.
Now I word-play moves on a page,
make moves on a different stage,
but my love for dance stays, always.

A Sonnenizio to Dance

I have always felt the joy of dance,
the playfulness and lightness when I danced.
I was a spontaneous, not well-trained dancer.
Now older and a non-dancer, I observe
and enjoy others out-dance my earlier attempts.
Any rhythms are danceable to me.

Even poetry can be dancy.
Perhaps hip-hop lyrics are the danciest.
With dancing there is a flowing,
free-expressing abundance of movement.
In accordance with innovative choreography,
there is an ascendance of the soul.

With guidance from dance lovers
poetry, music and motion find concordance.

Somewhere I Am Dancing

Somewhere in the cloudiness of a dream
I am with high school friends on a trip.
When I wake up, to my delight
my bone-on bone-arthritis vanished.
I move my legs without pain.
I stand to dance. I'm free.

The rest of the dream is a blur.
I can't recall the scenery or talk.
I remember the exhilaration of movement,
floating, free as an angel, ecstatic!
Even in the dream I am so grateful
for the gift of painless dance.

When I wake up here, I don't
even have to place my feet on the floor
to know I will hobble from the room.
I cry not for the pain only, but
for the dance dream lost.
Hope hangs heavy.

Choreographing the Day

This middling morning I awoke
with bed face and bed hair.
The crinkles and kinks smoothed
from my face in time.
A comb tamed some stray strands.

Time to choreograph the day
from task to task, place to place.
Dancing in my mind
when my body is not in rhythm.
The rituals, commitments,
the maintenance manual
of body and mind flow
into the day.

I check my We'Moon calendar.
It is a daily guide
to natural rhythms for women.
Printed on recycled paper
with soy-based ink.
I'm doing my small bit for the environment.
in each rectangled day-slot, words prompt.

After some feeding and reading
I check the day's demands
and usually write in any gaps,
putting on paper what the mind twirls.
Meter is like dance steps,
lines are like line dancing.
A poem is a playful dance
I choreograph with pleasure and passion.

My day is like contemporary dance
expressing emotions yearning to be free.
I studied modern dance when
I was lithe and limber.
Now I watch dancers with awe.
I stage each day to add dance movements
in my mind and in my schedule
always open to surprising moves.

Wind-Dancer

Let go and you're a dancer on the wind. Carolyn Myers

Like an autumnal leaf,
I hold on until time to let go,
but I am not bereft
when I let my thoughts flow.
      All energy is a subtle dancer.
      I want be a freelancer.

I hold on until time to let go
of thoughts, breath, this existence.
How long I have I do not know.
I'm trying to lessen my resistance.
      Life on Earth can be dark.
      I am ready to disembark.

But I am not bereft.
I'll try to stay in the light.
To do so I must be deft,
to move gracefully with insight.
      I have committed to stay
      to care, to teach, to sway.

When I let my thoughts flow,
I hope to rid myself of fear,
dwell on delight, service, show
love, be open for dances to appear.
      Regardless of the circumstance
      I want some part of me to dance.

All energy is a subtle dancer
moving in and out of form.
It becomes a life-enhancer.
Expression is not uniform.
      Everything is energy in motion.
      We are all part of this commotion.

I want to be a freelancer,
use freewill to create,
to be a life advancer,
to peacefully participate.
      Most of all I want to light-dance
      spread hope, give love a chance.

Daily Light

Sleepless in Corvallis

At eleven I went to bed as mostly usual
but I am unable to fall asleep.
Such a long stretch of sleeplessness is unusual
even with deep breathing and counting sheep.
My mind keeps grinding and racing
My thoughts are sleep chasing.

But I am unable to fall asleep
having to lie on my left side
and I have many issues to sweep
under my pillow where worries reside,
also my arthritic knees aching
and chilly, shivering flesh shaking.

Such a long stretch of sleeplessness is unusual
even staying up for Stewart and Colbert.
With some rituals and reflective perusal
sleep usually takes me in its care.
Time for creative dreaming,
with vivid images streaming.

Even with deep breathing and counting sheep
my body is uncomfortable, mind whirling.
I review concerns and hope to keep
dilemmas and a trente-sei's ideas twirling.
A carcinoma removed from right shoulder
makes me sore and my mood smoulder.

My mind keeps grinding and racing
I rub out doubt, plan new schemes.
wonder what commitments I'm spacing,
while gnawing concerns, exploring dreams.
My mother always said it's best
if you just relax and try to rest.

My thoughts are sleep chasing.
I go to the bathroom each hour,
find my brain and body pacing
until time to get up and shower.
Probably two hours sleep before I awoke.
I'm blaming unrest on a late diet Coke.

Heavy Matter   Light Matter

Sluggishly, after a restless sleep,
I lugged my heavy mind and body toward dawn.
After breakfast I return to bed, still lumpish.
I left 3-D for a less dense dream dimension.

I exist in a holographic-high-vibe type reality
wearing brown patterned pajamas, when
surprise guests appear in my backyard.
I need to get dressed to greet them..

I wander past a sleeping child in a crib
to fumble in a six-drawer bureau
to find a velvet, purple pantsuit to put on.
I rush to join our guests.

Downstairs in a bright-white walled,
multi-level house are the diva Deltas
- some sorority I do not belong to
but who I have let meet in my house.

I still have not found the original guests
when a decorator in that surreal place
tells me to go to a playroom loft
they had redecorated for me.

The centerpiece of the room is a green,
lighted, artificial Christmas tree
with enchanting new wooden hand-painted
ornaments like ones my Earth family made.

In the earthly plane our folk-artsy ornaments
dangle by red ribbons and hooks on a spiral dowel
tree hanging from the ceiling in an outdoor enclosed room.
There it is April and they still remain since Christmas.

This other-worldly tree has vibrant, new conceptions.
On the walls and tops of shelves and storage pieces splayed
more magical wooden creature ornaments. Some moved
          up and down like perpetual Jack-in-the-boxes
                    or animatronic figures dancing.
                              One a jubilant Santa with wings.

I looked out of the loft to a room with a vaulted ceiling.
Myriads of wooden ornaments wafted from the walls
and ceiling - seeming to fly all over the room
like solid fairies. They hung-out without supports.

I sensed different densities in this realm.
This home was awash with whimsy.
In this other world my anxiety lightened:
          where I dressed in purple pantsuit
                    entertained surprising guests
                              owned a light-hearted home redecorated
                                        with animating wooden ornaments.

When I woke the ornaments appeared exploded–
free from my earthly wooden ornaments
hooked to an unpainted dowel branch
captive of earthbound imagination.

I walked spritely to the lingering dowel tree.
I twirled the spiral– like a galaxy filled with stars.
Sun spilled through the window.
I released my shenpa.

Monday Morning Moodling

This morning I slept in.
I did not want to go to exercise class
I awoke at 10 to my chagrin
having wakened first at 6 alas.
Groggily I rushed to feed
while newspaper I blurrily read.

I did not want to go to exercise class
It's a video not a person any more.
So I will probably gain more mass.
No teacher makes it easy to ignore.
Tuesday/Thursday class has person in charge
Those days I am less likely to enlarge.

I awoke at 10 to my chagrin
I did not plan to sleep so late
but interesting dreams settled in
with tidbits to assimilate.
This reality rests and renews.
I wake up with discovered views.

Having wakened first at 6 alas
I knew my dreaming was not done.
Need still more sand through hour-glass
to reach my next curious destination.
I hold this reality focus in suspension
as I learn from another dimension.

Groggily I rushed to feed
same blueberries bouncing in yogurt.
With meds, that is all I need.
Still have to face the daily hurt.
Maybe that is why I stayed in bed
in cushioned, light world instead.

While newspapers I blurrily read
fail to lighten mind and soul,
reveal violence, inequality, greed,
I seek ways to make me whole.
I'll meditate in my red cape,
imagine a poem and for a while-- escape.

Lacking Legerity

Legerity: physical or mental quickness, nimbleness, agility

Couch potato today.
    Lackluster energy.
        Mind muddled by grief and worry.
            Body aching, straining to move.

Why not keep my legs up
    when placing them on the ground
        pains me to stand up?
            Icing chills and numbs.

Why not play mind games that aim
    at keeping playfulness alive
        avert turbulent thoughts
            perhaps provide respite of sleep.

Operating at low speed of mobility,
    what will speed up my metabolism of mind and body?
        Acceptance of low level productivity seems giving up
            any chance of feeling better.

        So I will gingerly rise from cushy couch,
    find some scrumptious dark chocolate,
trod toward the computer with stiffened steps
and seek solace in writing this poem with some degree of legerity.

The Stress List

Upon review of my stress list
to reduce stressors in my life,
this is to inform you
you did not make the cut.

This means my attachment
to you and your issues
must become detachment
and you must deal on your own.

When physical and emotional pain
become debilitating, sometimes
I have to focus on areas
of most importance to function.

My energies are strained.
I have not witnessed any tactics
I have tried in your behalf
have improved your situation.

I have concluded things will not change
for you until you want to change.
Wasted worry on my part is not
constructive to either of us.

My stress list is long.
My coping skills diminishing.
I must lighten my load
and help where it is most effective.

You are an important relationship
but the draining of connection
makes it necessary for me
to keep my distance at this time.

If some items on the list get resolved,
perhaps you will move up for reconsideration.
At the moment you do not seem to need my help.
If you do, find someone who tolerates deception.

You are checked off the list.
Checked out. Good luck.

The Fortune Cookie Says

Focus on long-term goals in the coming week.
but I have not met short term goals
even for today. Small goals loom like stumbling blocks
en route to fulfilling my bucket list.

I'll try taking one-at-a-time quick steps
until I can envision my long-term goal.
I might not live long enough to reach
completion of a distant project.
But one byte at a time I might finish
writing a book.

First I might decide if I have a long term goal
or many. What would it be
and is it up to me to achieve it?

Making a Mountain Out of a Mole Hole

A purple felt hat domes
on my sewing box.
mounds a mountain
on my dresser.

The hat warmed by head all winter.
a Christmas gift from my soft son.
The sewing box from my
needilly mother-in-law
lies unused like a coffin.

How can I protect my molded hat
from moths–a moth-safe place
to store it–not forgotten
like the sewing tools
that could mend the hat
if moths should snuggle inside.

I could flicker my overhead light
to attract them from my hat.
Moth trap tents and moth balls stink.
Electric zappers annoying.

Suffocating hats in a plastic bag
makes felt look shiny.
in a superficial way.
Perhaps a hat box like for elegant ladies.
But do they still sell them?
Plastic storage is not worthy of this hat.

I had better decide–spring is coming.
Moths could air-condition my hat.
I already have too many holes to fill.

Wormholes

*My dreams will pull me back to a place where a hole has opened....*Constance Eggers

Charcoal black bird blends
with parking lot asphalt
skittering between cars
with a tidbit in shiny beak.

Searching for a faraway nest
in a mall-ed desert,
the bird narrowly escapes
my chunk of blue metal.

My groceries gobbled
in shopping bags in the trunk
await opening into pots
and into mouths.

Wormholes on earth
and in space offer
the bird and me opportunities
for bite and byte.

The bird and I can dream
of opening places
where holes bring rebirth
to create and sustain us.

Blueberries

The blueberries bouncing in my already
blueberried, 0% milkfat, Greek yogurt
are from Argentina this week.
The Safeway clerk assured me
they had blueberries from somewhere
most of the time.
She wishes she could go to Argentina
when they inspect the crops.

Recently the blueberries were local,
some promised organic.
With the GMO bill not passing in Oregon
I will have no idea if the blueberries
are genetically modified
or where they come from
if not told by someone.

But I will take the risk
and not be P.C.
I will savor these exotic berries
bubbling my breakfast.
Blueberries also delightfully
found their way to flavor, with almonds,
the 72% dark chocolate bar,
product of Switzerland,
hiding in the file drawer
beside my alluring computer.

Sarah's Angel

Sarah struggles out of her truck,
cane clutched in hand
onto the Safeway parking lot.

I park beside her
in a handicapped space.
Both handicapped stickers dangle like wings.

She gives me an adorable angel
holding the word "friends" with three
mini-angels like beads on a bracelet.

Sarah was going to give me the angel
for my collection the next day
in exercise class...but I wouldn't be there.

I would be at a healing session
for my bone-on-bone arthritic knees.
She had one knee replaced recently.

I give Sarah a hug and assure her
we are indeed good friends.
She brings laughter to our class.

Both knee patients wobble our way
to our next destination. Angel in hand,
I face healing with added hope.

The Centenarian

Curved as the cane he hunches over,
an old man creeps across the crosswalk
toward the clinic.

I park in a handicapped spot
because of bone on bone arthritic knees
and walk unassisted toward the clinic.

Inside at the check-in counter
I see the man again. When he lifts his head,
I recognize it is Charles.

When I greet him, he says my name
and gives his regards to my husband,
his colleague for many years.

When asked his birth date,
he says 1914. He is 100!
I stepped away so he could make an appointment.

The young woman explained
she could fit him in, in an hour.
or he could come back another day.

Charles seemed to be having some trouble
processing his options. She was patient.
Finally, he said he'd come back in an hour.

I hoped we could talk if he waited,
but like light-drawn creatures
he tapped his cane toward the exit.

Charles, the dapper professor,
of culture and personality, world traveler,
tennis player, L.A. publicist and realtor–hobbled.

I told the woman behind the desk
I appreciated how thoughtfully she treated him.
She said, " Wow, he was 100!"

She had taken classes in the same department
where he taught at the university.
but she was not his student, until now.

My husband and I discussed
how to honor such a milestone.
Few of the current faculty know him.

We hosted a gathering about five years ago
which he attended, alert and engaging
to celebrate the department's 40th anniversary.

Charles is still driving, still moving.
Images of a once vibrant, youthful man shrivel.
My husband will call him before the chance crumbles.

Collecting Mini-Creatures

My mini-museum holds thousands of miniatures–
seasonal and permanent residents
on tables, shelves, dangling aloft.
Elves, fairies, angels, animals–
each perched with their own viewpoints.

These wise intuitive interlopers
communicate on their own Wii
(Wireless inanimate internet)
gossiping about the family and guests
and listening to electronic media
as they correspond
from rooms all over the house.

Immobility is not an issue,
if you are telepathic.
Their silent sentience is undetected
by the clueless mobile species
wandering in their midst.
They retain their own essence
regardless of differing perceptions.

I selected mini-creatures for my collection
due to inviting facial features, various media
or diverse artistic expression.
Each miniature of human imagination
might have a spark like our soul
residing invisibly as their essence.
A touch animates wave-lengths
of each creation to pulse in the universe.

When I stand facing the angels
to direct the Hallelujah chorus,
dance beside the fairy and elfin folk,
carefully prepare the seasonals
for hibernation in boxes,
I feel a special reverence for all life
no matter how still their life style.

Annalee Mobilitee

Dwell in possibility. Emily Dickinson

My mother collected Annalee Mobilitee--
wire- framed, felt-covered dolls with sweet faces
She passed on her meager collection to me.
To look at them–sadness erases.
   They dwell in my house every season.
   They bring serendipity beyond reason.

Wire-framed, felt-covered dolls with sweet faces--
hand-painted expressions of their features.
Around my home in diverse spaces
live these miniature animal and human creatures.
   They brighten my life every day,
   make festive every holiday.

She passed on her meager collection to me
which I enhanced when prices dropped.
Started in New Hampshire, China eventually
their allure to me has never stopped.
   Now I have hundreds of Mobilitee dolls
   to enhance collections of fairies and trolls

To look at them–sadness erases
I lead them in song, give each a view,
They are witnesses to joy that replaces
sadness for anyone entering this playful venue.
   Visitors get enchanted by my angels as well
   but adore the Annalee figures too, I can tell.

They dwell in my house every season,
follow celebrations with color and light.
lifting spirits to breeze on.
Always a source of daily delight
   Everywhere I look they bring a smile.
   I pause for gratitude a while.

They bring serendipity beyond reason
in the realms of surreality.
I know these dolls will please-on
after my brief stay in this reality.
   As I experience the possibility of now
   they make my now happier somehow.

Hosting House Guests

Before they appear at our welcoming door
we clean, we plan, we check-off our lists.
We wonder what changes they bring from last visit.

They arrive with eccentricities,
dietary needs. mobility concerns,
hauling luggage, excess baggage.

They expect entertainment, accommodations
for their spacial and emotional issues,
their circadian rhythms and schedules.

We provide a king-size or double bed,
handicapped equipped bathrooms, spritely
conversation, a shoulder to cry on, a hug.

We adapt to their requirements.
My husband tends to meals and beverages.
He is well-trained by cordial, social Yankee parents.

When family and friends visit, it is a puzzle.
How can we mesh the pieces into connection?
How can we enjoy individuality with harmony?

Dirty Dogs Doggerel

Our granddaughter was dog-sitting two dogs.
Zeu$ is her Maltese. Arwen belongs to Dad.
Dogs' misbehavior she catalogues.
Their doggy actions make her mad.
She cannot work on a college term paper
when all around her the dogs caper.

Zeu$ is her Maltese. Arwen belongs to Dad.
He is at a conference in Kentucky. She's in charge.
Their annoying antics became very bad.
Her temper bloomed very large.
A thunder storm sent dogs into panics.
Rain caused several dirty dog antics.

Dog's misbehavior she catalogues.
Dogs bark in thunderous fears.
She calls Dad with monologue.
The whole house is in arrears.
Sticks in bed, mud paw-prints floors
every time they go outdoors.

Their doggy actions make her mad.
She can't concentrate and clean,
as dirty dogs in grubby, muddy parade
makes her studying progress unforeseen.
She finally decides she can't cope.
Her Grandpa's rescue her best hope.

She cannot work on a college term paper
and meet dogs and housework needs.
She finds her patience begins to taper.
"Come Grandpa for doggy care", she pleads.
He comes to walk dogs twice a day
and for three nights agrees to stay.

When all around her dogs caper,
she gets fed-up and finally leaves.
As she becomes the dog-escaper,
Grandpa comes and he relieves.
Her term paper does get done.
Sun comes out for everyone.

Ring Tones

Night Calls

Calls
in
the night
bring nightmares.
We wake from deep dreams.
We're hollowed, full of fear, rings long.

Morning Calls

Yawn
to
awake..
Less a jolt,
Light becomes our hope.
Dreams from naps prompt us to rise– fast.

Day Calls

Now
we're
awake--
reminder
an interruption.
We hang up to resume routine.

Call Waiting

We can't call out from cell or land line phone.
Callers can call us but we can't respond.
Solicitors still won't leave us alone
We can't call for help. Can't get beyond
the dial tone which in monotone hums.
I sit and twiddle my thumbs.

Callers can call us, but we can't respond.
We can't call them back with a question.
I can't swish a Comcast fairy wand
to give them a technical suggestion.
I use the land line. Husband uses a cell.
Now both phones are not working well.

Solicitors still won't leave us alone
with early morning rings and silent pauses.
When they do not answer, I always groan
at their tricky gimmicks and scam causes.
But if we try to reach out for help,
no one will hear our urgent yelp.

We can't call for help. Can't get beyond
receiving and not sending.
Somehow have we been conned?
Is there some bill pending?
Our payments are automatic.
Why am I so melodramatic?

The dial tone which in monotone hums
provides no lyrics to waft through air.
We will have to wait for what repair comes
for we aren't calling anywhere.
We listen for the phones to ring,
with whatever news they bring.

I sit and twiddle my thumbs.
The cell finally makes connection.
My tweedle--dee and tweedle--dums
only made the cell selection.
My land line phone remains unhooked
I ponder what I've overlooked.

Checking-in on My Chakras

After checking the Internet for definitions,
purposes, healing techniques and colors,
I find I need a more diverse diet, flexibility
to do yoga, running, dancing–deep breathing.

Since I like blueberries and chocolate,
the Third-Eye Chakra gets my best dietary rating.
The Crown Chakra suggests breathing exercises
which I try with meditation techniques.

All the other chakras with food not
in my diabetic diet, or desiring mobility
like dancing, yoga positions, habitual running
make my bone-on-bone arthritic knees cringe.

Checking the purposes of these energy centers
I saw areas of improvement. Not all appear probable.
My acupuncturist knows where they are
and my masseuse finds some sore spots.

Root Chakra at base of spine is red.,
deals with foundation, feeling grounded,
survival issues. I have been considered
loosely attached to the planet so must tighten the tether.

Sacral Chakra in lower abdomen 2 inches below navel
and 2 inches in is orange, concerned with connection,
sense of abundance, ability to accept others and new experiences,
well-being, pleasure, sexuality. Mixed performance for me.

Solar Plexus Chakra in the upper abdomen stomach area
is yellow, effects ability to be confident, in control of our lives,
self-worth, self-confidence, self-esteem. My weight suggests
some issues here, as well as still striving to meet goals.

Heart Chakra is green in center of chest above heart,
concerns ability to love, joy and inner peace. Now since
I have learned from heart break and am learning detachment
from judgment, I am calmer and making progress here.

Throat Chakra is blue and located in the throat.
Communication, self-expression of feelings and truth
stem from here. As a teacher, writer, logophile,
I am trying to be skillful with words. Success–varies.

Third-Eye Chakra is indigo, in the center of the forehead
between eyes. Intuition, imagination, wisdom, ability to think
and make decisions originate from here. My favorite chakra.
My love of blueberries and dark chocolate gives me brownie points.

Crown Chakra is violet or white at the top of the head,
site of inner and outer beauty, our connection to spirituality,
pure bliss. I cleanse it with salt, have done shamanic work,
collected thousands of angels, yet remain spiritual not religious.

My chakra check list reveals I have a lot of maintenance
and healing to do. When I get into the nitty-gritty, I see
many areas to improve on. Chakra means "wheel".
How long can I keep rolling on patched tires about to go flat?

Researching, using boji balls, crystals, color therapy,
meditation tapes, revising viewpoints, exercising,
using consultants-- all could help me heal and increase movement.
Maybe I can twirl my chakras into spinning tops, whirling dervishes!

Light-Hearted

Flumadiddle

utter nonsense, worthless frill.   Dictionary.com

Flumadiddle is in the eyes of the beholder,
Chomping dark chocolate, some might consider
a nonsensical, worthless frill, but
these dark chocolate covered blueberries
are worth making a fool over.
Some of my word-play is flumadiddle.

Much of our planetary past does not make sense
and supposedly solid facts evaporate
with new evidence, currently approved.
How many humans utter nonsense,
much of their lives, lured
by baubles and worthless frills.

Some productions are deliberate comedy,
slapsticks for laughs which is nonsense
for an uplifting purpose. Worthless frills
are for the rich as the poor can't afford them.
Inequality allows some people to flumadiddle
more than others. A downward purpose.

Perhaps Earthlings's brain cannot process
all the cosmos offers, so they invent or convolute data
in ways that appear ridiculous to less frivolous beings.
Some believers follow flumadiddle metaphysics.
Some politicians postulate preposterous policies.
We all can be a fumbling flumadiddle sometimes.

Not Performing as One

Walking into a theater,
with the play script
in my hand, I search for
others in this play.

As they gather beforehand
they tell us they have changed
the roles.   The role I was expecting
was changed to read
the role of One.

I looked for my script
to learn the new lines,
but the blue cover with white printing
was missing.
Frantically I looked for the script.
A row of readers had their scripts
and on a a nearby stage,
actors held their scripts, reading their lines
before the performance began.

Noone seemed to have my missing script.
I went to an adjoining room
filled with the soon-to-be audience
chatting, drinking wine, indifferent
to the panicking actor searching
for a script to perform as One.

Then the play began, I raced
back to the line of readers,
the audience laughed when a line
for One was not read.
I scrambled for a script
from the player beside me,
but I had no idea where in the play
we were and could not find
the lines for One.

The play must go on- despite
One so flustered, I woke up.

Earworms

Earworms are the catchy,
annoyingly repetitive tunes
that get stuck in your head.
Like earphones you forget
to take off replaying songs.
Some rap, rock and roll
and other songs seem
on continual replay when
supposedly listening on
some technical device.

People with greater cognitive function
experience earworms
for shorter duration than less
cognitive capable people,
scientists say. Some volunteers
tried to focus on another task but
it had to be neither too challenging
nor too simple to unstick a sticky tune.

A website claimed chewing
on cinnamon gum can keep a song
from getting gummed up in one's head.
So experiments with chewing gum
determined jaw's up and down
motion while chewing does help...some.
Apparently the jaw affects memory
and ability to imagine music.

Other volunteers pressed the "q"
on a keyboard whenever a certain song
popped into their head.   But maybe
you can use these auditory images
to bore yourself to sleep,
syncopate your exercise routine,
choreograph a dance marathon,
accompany a monotonous job,
replace deep breathing in a different rhythm,
background music for your visual images
or slurring sounds preventing sleep.
At times your brain seems an orchestra of sound
and you are not the conductor.

Though the tunes change this is not a new phenomena.
Guess I'd better choose my music more soothingly
to give brain and body a break—metaphorically.

Obitchuary

Another flawless saint
loving and beloved,
by numerous fans,
a truly angelic person
has gone home to God,
laid to rest
in the newspapers and on-line.

A trusted or tactful friend
or family member
praised the passing
with feathered, fabricated facts.
None of the abusive, evil people
ever seem to die.

What's between the lines
of these often delusional details?
This raises the question–
"The devil got your tongue?"

The truth is often spoken to therapists
and by victims who rarely
speak out at funerals
and by absence of grief.

How about an honest obitchuary
calling into account the lapses
in character and achievements
of the deceased?

Who would dare to write it?
If you pay enough, they probably
would print it, along
with the deceased's requests
for donations to a favorite charity

Honesty on the tombstone?
Here lies (name or alias)
drug addict, sex pervert,
manipulative, mooching,
greedy, violent, frequently jailed
son of a bitch.

Perhaps dishonored in life, in death
there is no one to write an obitchuary
or provide a cemetery plot.

Triskaidekaphobia

A fear or a phobia concerning the number 13. Dictionary.Com

Today is February 13th
the day before Valentine's Day.
Ancient superstitions
persist in Anthropocene.

I admit I have been oblivious
of the date most of today
until I had to write a check
for my massage.

A friend treated for lunch
and paid with a credit card.
I gave her a manuscript
for my next book to prepare for print.

Now that I am aware
it is Friday the 13th
will it change my game plan
or luck for this day?

Already I am thinking ahead
to Valentine's Day. I wrote
a Sardine Sonnet for hubby
to go with six cans of Sardines.

Love should trump fear
any day really. Thirteen
is a number-- first teen year
which causes some parental fear.

Omnishambles

My exercise program is in omnishambles.
My low impact exercise could have levity,
does not have to be bogged in a warm water pool
where I chug chlorine, scratch rashes,
endure clarity and temperature malfunctions,
swamp smell and fungal infection;
take too many showers, un-dress and re-dress repeatedly.

I could return to land exercises without the jump-jarring,
joints out of joint, rubber band flexibility demands,
make modifications to aching routines--.
But why not fly?

I could design a trapeze like Cirque de Soleil.
I could hook a narrow swing on ropes from the ceiling.
The seat can be soft fabric like fleece or quilted.
I can spread it out like a chair
or bunch it up to ride like on a swayback horse.

Legs can swing easier together to and fro
or split straddling the swing to ski or do splits.
Try jacks and free-floating foot movements,
swish those arthritic knees about
and never touch the ground.
Hold the ropes for security or
try balancing free-handed on your high ride.

I'd like to be able to lower it also
perhaps with pulleys or zip cords,
Maybe bungee cords to bounce.

I could do seated exercises feet flat on floor.
Arms shrugging, spreading, lifting
pulling even with weights.
I'm comfortable in diverse positions.

When done, I zap the swing
to splat against the ceiling,

With some design decisions
the fabric could look like a ceiling light shade
or meager art attempt of the Sistine Chapel
or just let it droop like a smile.

Hysterically Naked

Strip down to bathing suit,
put on swim shoes and gloves
shower, drip and dry
then redress. Maybe several times a day.

What if the next evolutionary step
had an internal temperature regulation system.
You could go naked all year–everywhere.
Thermally adjusted with free mobility.

For those who like color, be comfortable in your own skin
you could project designs onto the epidermis
from your brain like tattoos without pain
just by thought like virtual reality.

You could change your fashion
anytime you want-- no wash or wear
without the hassle of dressing, stressing over make-up
or whether an outfit still fits or is out of style.

If your weight fluctuates- no problem.
Your mind can alter patterns more fitting.
You could use body hair for texture
or de-nude skin for smoother contours.

What fun to change outfits at will.
Nipples the centers for daisies or sunflowers.
Moles, warts, scars, skin tags all camouflaged–
all illusions of your creativity.

I am tired of dressing up and down for occasions.
I'm tired of layering and taking off garments.
I'd rather be thermally reliable, wear my own style
and really express myself regardless of fad or fashion.

This evolution might not come in this lifetime.
Tattoos do not have the same appeal
as glowing, glistening internally generated art
dazzling every curve and protuberance.

Until my dream wardrobe is mainstream,
I will fumble with fastenings, openings,
encumbered limbs, covered body parts,
but I am thinking of my nude fashion statement.

At the moment I am hysterically naked
with jiggling bits and globular bounces.
No disguises can cover-up my blemishes.
I laugh at my imperfections and future reincarnational dreams.

Shapify

More dense than a hologram
3-D rather than 2-D "selfie "
I can create a replica of myself
by additive manufacturing,
controlled by a computer robot
adding layers to create a statue
reproducing myself in different sizes,
different materials for different prices.

To create a "shapie" sculpture stand
in the center of a circular platform   surrounded by white backdrops
with four scanners attached.
rotate 360 degrees
and voila-- in 12 seconds the
scanned 3-D image has captured
data sent to cloud-based server.
The figurine is composed off-site
using a 3-D color printer.
About a week later, the "shapie" is formed.
You can create portraits for gifts
or document change How about play figures?
You do not look better than you look.
Guess I should have created
my "shapie" about 50 pounds ago.
But then it was not invented.
What a great memorial statue
to gaze at rather than ashes.
A more realistic depiction of yourself
or a loved one, a reflection of a wedding,
special events, graduations
to place on a shelf or table
to remember all the good times.
3-D printing can create many devices
to improve health, new art, reproductions
in many materials, to replace body parts,
enhance education, research, aircraft, cars,
construction, communication, home computers,

even a 3-D printer in the Space Station
and to make coral reefs for the ocean.
can even customize food like chocolate.
Wow- my own dark chocolate dispenser!
Few limits on its applications.
I prefer artistic and healthy uses
rather than guns and violent capacities.

I'd love to create a 3-D poem   "Shapies" can expand reality creatively
Maybe in color, a shape poem,   Human imagination is boundless.

Ode to True Blue

1991 Blue Geo Metro

Tomorrow we turn you in
for True Blue Two
She is not car kin
more high-tech than you.

You have been my pal
for 24 years.
Few bad times to recall
very few tears.

Your parts are wearing out
pretty much like mine.
I have little doubt
you're parts gold mine.

Too many things
don't work anymore.
Issues of safety brings
me to thoughts I deplore.

I will miss my cute car
my favorite color blue
all the true blue you are
and your frailties too.

My Obama sticker,
the dents, pealing paint.
will go. We'll dicker
for another saint.

I'll drive a blue Honda Fit
all shiny, screens, cameras too
with buttons all over it,
telling me what to do.

I won't have to shift
or use a door key
my driver's seat can lift,
so I can see.

I had trouble getting in
your obstinate, low door.
You had trouble letting in
anyone anymore.

I loved your style
your blemishes, flare
and all the while
noticed everywhere.

My family and friends
loved you too.
When friendship ends
and travels are few,

we all mourn the loss
of a car so true
for a car with new gloss
not patinaed like you.

I remember our good times
and our bad
yet my deep love chimes
and I am sad.

We could still donate you
or make you electric car
someone could renovate you–
but so far.

Tomorrow we will turn you in
for a safer, still blue Fit
I'll come to love your car kin
and make of best of it.

But farewell beloved True Blue
you have served me well.
I will always remember you
in my heart you'll dwell.

Imperfect Fit

I am not sure my new Honda Fit
is the perfect fit for me.
It fit all the criteria for a new car
blue, 4-door, automatic, fuel-efficient.
I can get in easily, operate windows,
no keys, adjust seat so I can see
and get in and out with some grace.
I love the cameras for backing.
More bells and whistles than I will
ever use or know how to.
This blue car glistens in the sun.
I'll call her True Blue Two.

True Blue is a 1991 Geo Metro:
patina-ed by pealing paint,
dented, creaky doors and windows,
stick shift a tad wobbly.
Keys do not unlock doors or trunk
reliably, seat too low to exit
without a groan.   Yet when
we cleaned her out the seats
looked in good condition, she
glowed from the car wash.
Oil helped some of her joints.
It was as if she were pleading
with me to keep her. I do have
tears in my eyes and heart.
I am not emotionally fit for a new car.
I am not a technological fit either.

The dealer wanted to pay $100.
We said no. We'd donate her
to Public Broadcasting or convert
her into an electric car. A man
wants to see her tomorrow and
pay $500 cash if her likes her.
I will not sell her to anyone
who does not love her like I do
or I'll have a fit.

I named True Blue Two in her honor.
Despite her glitz and glamour,
techie-tricks, she has to fit
not just my driving needs, but
my expectations for a comfortable,
safe ride, growing affection, for she
is my last car until I am unfit to drive,
the car I'll drive into the sunset,
the car I will pass on to someone else
who is deemed a perfect fit to care for her.

My True Blue, the 1991 Geo Metro

For 24 years you were True Blue.
We had some bumps and glitches too
but through it all, I loved you.

Your trunk studs failed, bonked my head.
I went to class though head bled,
ended in hospital instead.

Driving from Salem on the highway
the clutch seemed to give way.
No cell, left in traffic to pray.

Your doors got stuck, won't unlock.
Sent to Midwest to get right stock
No radio and off-time clock.

Windows hard, made shoulders hurt.
Dent population had growth spurt.
Getting in and out made me curt.

The stick shift wobbled- enough
I reached limit of aging stuff.
But loyalty stopped my bluff.

On a trip we rented a Kia Soul.
I realized you had taken a toll
on me and Honda Fit topped poll.

Reluctantly we will part ways
I will be grateful always
for our many vagabond days.

Fast Thoughts in the Slow Lane

My thoughts race, but movement slow
My body's on idle, gearing down to stop.
Somehow I've lost my get up and go.
Travel too slow to attract a cop.
This engine needs an overhaul.
Must rev up for journey overall.

My body's on idle, gearing down to stop.
Fueled by sugar and not enough green,
I feel my belly about to pop
in my no longer lean machine.
Sluggish, I need an oil change
so I can increase my mobility range.

Somehow I've lost my get up and go.
Need maintenance in body shop.
I want my limbs and systems to flow,
to keep my thinking tiptop.
The traffic gets heavy and enraging.
I prefer rest areas clean and engaging.

Travel too slow to attract a cop.
No speeding tickets for me.
Would love to dance to hip hop
or any dance gracefully.
I'd like to move without aching.
What fun to do booty shaking!

This engine needs an overhaul--
an efficient fuel injection system,
good steering to drive it all,
an older model with wisdom.
negotiating turns, varying speeds
and still get what this vehicle needs.

Must rev up for journey overall
as my equipment's quickly aging.
Must meet demands before curtain call
with best script and staging.
I'll aim to be a blue Volvo
aiming to steal the show.

Shopping in the Fast Lane

No leaning on the shopping cart.
I have a hectic schedule today.
        I'm taking the fast lane.

The energized, motorized scooter
is unplugged and ready to go.
After pondering and fumbling levers and buttons
        I'm taking the fast lane.

I zip over to the deli for my regular
super kale salad and baked chicken parts,
packaged and prepared for quick meal prep.
        I'm taking the fast lane.

Refills of sweet and salty snacks
for my perpetual buffet to propel writers,
to unscramble Scrabble players–for them
        I'm taking the fast lane.

As I cruise down the aisles
careful not to bruise or rundown shoppers,
impale on edgy shelves, topple produce or cans,
I must not lead-foot when
        I am taking the fast lane.

Once I careened through Cabela's--
zooming through coat racks, arrowing aisles,
whirling wheelies like a merry-go-round.
My family were not amused while
        I am taking the fast lane.

Back in Safeway, on my current trip
I go through the 15-item fast lane,
pause purring hotrod,
re-plug the race car before I leave.
        I hobble the slow lane to my Fit.

My Knees

My knees were bending boughs
pumping swings, dancerly,
athletic, jumped rope.

My knees now are rusty hinges
not yet metal-ized, just stone-bone
attached to failing supports.

My knees don't kneel,
remain stiff, almost robotic,
cuddle pillows, ache for props.

My knees slathered with pain cream,
braced with elasticize bands with magnetic coils,
aided by ice packs, probe the core of the problem.

My knees lean on grocery carts,
strut with cane and walker, but best of all
relax in a pushed, cushy wheelchair.

Healing With a Shaman

The shaman places three, oblong, faceted crystals- strategically,
uses an eagle feather to swish energy and breath,
blows in my crown chakra removes blockages
until green energy exits through my feet–cleansing.
My aura repaired from tears exudes colorful patterns.
Boji stones balance my bone-on- bone knees.
CDs calm and induce clarity through meditations.
A sheer turquoise cloth covers me in healing hue.
Breathing exercises enhance flow. His hands raise frequency.
Smudging clears air and my soul. Metal, triangular talisman hopes.
Natural creams reduce pain. Herbal pills help cure.
Salt washes crown chakra. Texts prepare me for new perceptions,
a new way of shifting energies
for a multidimensional outlook.

Becoming a Lighter Being

Rather than being a weighty, milky,
cow-ish carcass type woman,
I'd like to be a lighter being
living on light in a lighter world.

I need to diet dark
(with the exception of dark chocolate),
fill up with lighter fare
for body, mind and spirit.

In dualistic light/dark experiences
keeping one's light on
without dark-dousing is hard.
Light/heavy is just as challenging.

I lust for light.
I'm passionate about the positive.
Come on homo luminous hunk,
let's make love in a bright realm.

Stop and Go

Percentages

*Ninety-nine percent of your thoughts are a complete waste of time. They do
nothing but freak you out.*   Michael Singer

What freaky odds! Wow!
Not a fan of statistics
but such inequality goes –pow!
to all things altruistic.
My math is faulty. I question technique
to gather such "facts". We are unique.

Not a fan of statistics
I have no confidence in such "facts".
How do they determine thought characteristics
and what freakiness thought exacts?
        I pursue thought with curiosity
        and try to focus on creativity.

But such inequality goes–pow
into 99 percent of anything,
like Occupy movement now
protesting for justice, advocating
        more equitable distribution
        of access to any institution.

To all that's altruistic,
I side with the 99 percent also.
Our thoughts are pluralistic,
can include one percent to show
        some consensus that works for 100 percent
        for sustainability and what's resilient.

My math is faulty, I question technique
of determining percentage of any thought,
whether communal or an individual peek
at what is freaky or what we ought
        to explore creatively to enhance progress
        to move forward and not regress.

To gather such "facts"-- we are each unique--
just what facet was tested? How do they find
all the data on topics they seek.
all that lurks in humankind's mind?
       We are all one and not a percent.
       My thoughts not numbered or a quotient.

Conswervative

A typo created this new word to ponder.
Would we swerve con or pro?
Left or right views I wonder?
It would be fun to probe or know.
        A con swerve could be progressive
        or a con swerve could be regressive.

Would we swerve con or pro
toward the center or to extremes,
for progress or status quo,
enhancing or squishing dreams?
        Will we remain on static course?
        Will swerving be better or worse?

Left or right views I wonder
would be the trend if we swerve?
Will we budget or squander?
Will we touch a global nerve?
        If our planetary goals veer,
        can we still remain here?

It would be fun to probe or know
what benefits can come with change,
which direction our destiny will go,
are the results within our range?
        Stereotypes or people's viewpoints
        could be un-labeled for new points.

A con swerve could be progressive,
a shift to openness, more equality, fairness,
a way of being more impressive,
to be more active with more awareness.
        Conserve as protection, not inaction,
        to get things done, positive reaction.

Or a con swerve could be regressive
as against progressive, more sustainable choices.
Planetary survival needs to be digressive
to work together despite diverse voices.
        Conswervative can mean making best decisions
        before we run out of options and revisions.

Hisstory

It is bad enough the record of people's past
is called his story filled with violence
and speculation, leaving out her story
much of the time for "heroic" hissy fits.

But it becomes hisstory when inaccurate assessments
of what really went on is misinterpreted.
slanted with biases that become ingrained
in our misunderstanding.

Hi story to what might have actually existed.
As our techniques and instruments improve
we have a harder time
following the chronological line we were told.

Too many ooparts; prehistoric objects
with technological advancement out of sync
with what we believed was possible.
Maybe alienstory–landed E.T.'s.

Perhaps many civilizations came and left
either by extinction by mishandling resources
or taking resources to seed other planets.
We could be starseeds. Maybe starstory.

Ooparts re-think our past possibilities.
challenge our current knowledge,
open alternative theories.
Each of us can choose our interpretations.

150,000 year old radioactive iron pipes
dated by thermoluminescence found in China
lead under a lake bed and on the shore.
8 % of the material could not be identified.

Global pyramids, piles of megaton stone,
oopart inventions, engineering,
enhance heretical beliefs.
make us want to hiss at historians.

Our past becomes more mythical,
almost fictional, and our future sci-fi,
defying conventions and ways of knowing.
Mysteries of the universe leave us starry-eyed.

Expanding Human Rights

Human rights are women's rights and women's rights are human rights.
Hillary Clinton

When I was about six I cut off my blonde curls
and announced I was now David.
My brother was allowed to get dirty
play ball games and climb trees so
I had decided to be a boy.

My mother was in shock, but my hair grew in.
Still in dresses, I came home from kindergarten
as if I had gone to a mud pit. I was groomed
to become more feminine and knuckle under
what was expected of a good girl.

I was bound in ribbons in long tresses, dresses,
expected to act lady-like-- quiet and clean.
As I grew, I wore itchy crinolines
under umbrella-ed skirts to school,
learned to formal dance in scratchy net gowns.

In rebellion in the late fifties, girls
decided to wear their skirts higher.
When the principal commented on my attire
I said, " You wouldn't know if you weren't looking."
He backed off, as other boys found if they bothered me.

I was expected to wear hats, gloves, heels,
uncomfortable dresses on many occasions.
Birth control was not available, so when birth control pills
came out in college, two brilliant women died of blood clots
as the dosage was too high. They were unequally married.

I buckled at the clothing and evolved into pants,
tossed heels and dressed in comfortable clothes.
Much easier to teach, raise kids without
people peeking under my skirts.
I became a staunch feminist.

I was encouraged to be a nurse, secretary,
teacher or airline stewardess in high school.
Few sports available. Certain jobs-- off limits.
Equal rights amendment failed.
We have made some progress-- not enough.

When in graduate school I was called too ambitious,
expected to join the Putting Hubby Through group.
These women worked and hubbies ditched them at graduation.
I learned to keep within one college degree of partner,
support other women to be what they want to be.

I rejected the confines of traditional religions
as too male hierarchical, not giving women power
of choice over their own bodies and lives.
I advocated changes in the law to advance women.
Woman need to be free to think for themselves.

When teaching, writing or editing,
I always encouraged individual expression
to creatively push boundaries, question.
I know women are not only equal to men
but in many cases far surpass them.

Human rights are women's rights
but the rights of all humanity could use
an upgrade toward justice, compassion,
peace, harmony and greater equality for all--.
each climbs the tree of humanity..

International Women's Day 2014

After preaching equality and justice for women
to the choir, they will have He for She rallies
of men supporting women. But why
has it taken so long for both genders
to equally respect each other?

Huge relapses and gaps with grim statistics
exist all over the world. Violence
bleeds both sexes. Not enough bandages.
Not enough change of beliefs
in religions and cultures.

Supposedly young adults tend
to be more tolerant, nonreligious,
politically independent.
Will we move fast enough to prevent
global collapse and work together?

Picking Holly on the Winter Solstice

Picking holly from our front yard trees
is a prickly affair between heavy rains in algid air.
Red berries cluster abundantly amid sharp leaves.
My clippers snip the ends of the lower branches.

Two trees--one regular and one variegated
drop sheared offerings to a paper bag snare.
They will decorate our family's festival of light tables,
slither within candles and holiday tableware.

My thoughts turn to Newtown, Connecticut
where there will be many empty chairs
this darkled season of sorrow.
The berries spill like drops of blood.

It is the day some say the world will end,
though I chose a new age beginning.
More Mayan calendar days were found.
yet many devastating prophecies remain.

In Newtown makeshift memorials
with candles, flowers, toys, messages
provide light and compassion,
elicit 26 acts of kindness worldwide.

The holly splays and surrounds our candlesticks
and seasonal miniatures, many wearing red.
Our tables become altars as we light candles
for hope, peace, comfort for all celebrations of light.

Power Promises

High winds and rain storm blew out power
when a tree fell on a transmission line.
In the dark with only gray-light from a sky-light,
I fumble to find a small flashlight
to guide me to candles–tea candles eight white and one blue,
a red heart, mismatched candles on candlesticks
and a small, plastic, battery-powered angel
who glowed in six rotating colors.
Surrounded by flickering light I read for several hours
until the fixed power returned.

Near midnight I watched a replay of the Newtown vigil–
a gathering of grievers
for twenty first graders and six adults at Shady Hook school
gunned down by a deranged young man.
Clergy of many faiths, a Selectwoman, Governor Malloy
and President Obama stressed compassion, love
and support for the community and mourners..
Obama promised to use his power to help.
He questioned if we were powerless to make changes
so such violence does not kill others unable to escape madness.
How do we keep bright-eyed, innocent children safe?

The Amish school children, Aurora theater-goers, Columbine High School,
Virginia Tech and an ever-expanding list of victims
of assault weapon havoc by crazed young men.
The day Obama heard about the Newtown deaths
was the worst day of his tenure.
" Are we really prepared to say that we are powerless in the face
of such carnage, that the politics are too hard? he asks.

Outside the Newtown High School auditorium and around town
make-shift memorials of clusters of candles, teddy bears and toys,
photographs and sorrowful messages from around the world.
Inside an outraged, tear-fighting President says:
"Are we prepared to say that such violence on our children year after year
is somehow the price of our freedom?

Near the beginning of his talk he listed the names of the adults
killed in the attack, some shielding children.
Near the end, he intoned the names of the children
as the audience sobbed with people worldwide.

When will the weaponless be empowered?
        Gun sales continue to rise.
        Mental Health services remain underfunded.
        Politicians puzzle over a plan of what to do.

Darkness prevails. We are unsafe.
        I re-light sputtering candles
        despite restored electric power.
        Only I have power over me.

Hamba Kahle

Zulu for "go well".

The world mourns Nelson Mandela.
World Leaders and citizens gather for tributes
for the freedom fighter against apartheid.

In Newtown, Connecticut one year after massacre
of 20 children and six teachers, mourners
request the media stay at bay.

In Portland Oregon small memorials for mall
shooting victims as their loved ones mourn
and like Newtown seek gun control.

There is no easy walk to freedom
either in Africa or America.
Pathways paved in blood.

Passing the Buck

The economy has gone to crap.
Global warming lets climates sap.
Let politicians take the rap.

Women rights have taken a dive
Religious wars are kept alive.
Let politicians take the rap.

Housing loans cause foreclosures
Wall street deals lack disclosures
Let politicians take the rap.

Schools are going to pot.
Greater gap between haves and nots.
Let politicians take the rap.

Less taxes for the one percent.
Illegals come that legals resent.
Let politicians take the rap.

Will yammering about democracy,
look at citizens' liberty?
Let politicians take the rap.

Give responsibility to pro-choice.
See everyone has a voice.
Let individuals fill the gap.

Common Song

At the baseball All-Star Game
Marc Anthony revealing facial tics
tries to make our National Anthem singable
with pauses and embellishments.

Women with wardrobe malfunctions
and skimpy costumes
lead spectators of other sports
who stand and place hands over hearts.

Audiences adapt tune to ranges
they can reach. The variations
can be monotone to laughably off-key.
A better score would be more winning.

The words are more militant
than patriotic. Many forget lyrics.
Why not "America the Beautiful"
or "This Land is My Land."

Other National Anthems sound melodic
even not knowing the language.
Their songs' tones appear more accessible.
Our common song is uncommonly difficult.

Soulful?

My husband tells a friend
who writes and lectures about the soul,
he does not think he has one.
He just thinks he'll die and compost.
If he indeed has one, he would prefer
to blink out-- not have an eternal commitment.
If the cosmos is expanding and they need
souls they can create new ones.
They probably have enough without him.

Our son says the Buddhists
do not believe in souls
and just return to replenish the earth.
My husband is an agnostic environmentalist
but probably will not become a Buddhist.
Lots of opinions to consider.

Recently I read that a big batch of souls
burst from the Great Central Sun Alcyone
to scatter souls, sentient energy sparks,
throughout the cosmos, to experience
many forms in many existences.
We each have a soul-bit from this Creator.
(There may be many Source Creators).

These souls relay experiences in all kinds
of cosmic experiments to libraries.
We are like reporters- journalists of souls.
Each oversoul can splinter, facet or slice
to increase access to multidimensional,
simultaneous lives occurring Now.

Our concept of time is limited as
is our 3-D, duality equipment.
I am aware of being an Earthling
on a low-vibrational planet.
I struggle for positivity, peace,
harmony in a love-based universe.

I believe in angels and guides,
stardust seeding by E.T. beings.
Some people have otherworldly
abilities I do not have. I am trying
to raise my frequency to contact
other dimensions to see if I can confirm
some of my suspicions and what
I have been told could actually be true.
I am unaffiliated from organized religion,
so I need to try another spiritual or stellar approach.

Apparently my soul has 14
simultaneous expressions
and only one is on Earth.
I'd like to know what I am doing elsewhere.
My dreams occasionally give clues.

I think I am a cosmic collaborator
who has had multitudinous lives
all over the galaxies and universes.
Some intuitives have told me magical tales.
But some say our consciousness
is all an illusion and reality
only appears real. If so,
if we create our reality, why not create
a happy one- constructive and compassionate?

Many believe we should be preparing
for a 5th dimensional shift to the New Earth.
Reports are we will be in light bodies,
environmentally low impact, harmonic paradigm
in a love Utopia. The New Earth is heavenly.
Some proclaim if we raise our frequencies
and fulfill some rigamarole we can take
our bodies with us for recalibration on
an E.T. space ship. This is part of a galactic
renewal project so Earth can undergo
a purification cleansing, restoration, rehabilitation.
Humans have been polluting, destroyers
who need to go elsewhere so Gaia can heal.

Apparently in recent decades how this shift
will happen, the timing and procedures changed.
If I am needed to assist, I hope I am ready.
I can go in or out of body. I can leave all behind
as I explore my options for more soul lives.
All this is unimaginably complex.
Whatever is in store, I'm sure my husband and I
will be surprised, no matter what we believe.

The Light Switch

You turn me on and off like a light switch
depending on your current situation.

When you want me to enlighten-- you lift up.
When you want to keep me in the dark-- you push down.

But it's often unclear to me what switch
you will make, if any, in the energy flow.

Sometimes I am unaware of outages
until you flip the switch in daylight.

Disconnected, I wonder when repairs
will be made. I suspect your wattage.

Since constancy of connection is in doubt,
I find I seek light places-- with others.

Shades of Light

Darkness

In the dark light peeks through
       as moonlight   starlight
       candlelight   streetlights
       headlights   traffic lights
       window glow   neon show
We seek illumination in the dark.

In the dark about situations
       good or bad   happy or sad
       controlled or not   cold or hot
       relationships crumble   opportunities fumble
       unknowable or knowable
We seek resolutions when in the dark.

In the dark about the cosmos
       each a debater on the creator
       each wants to be shown if we are alone
       each has fervid requests while on our quests
       each attempts to understand we might not be in command.
We strive for cosmic meaning in the dark.

In the dark about my purpose
       Why am I here? To face fear?
       What should I be doing? What service accruing?
       If I succeed will I know before I go?
       Why am I in this place, part of human race?
I crave light when living in the dark.

Flickering Lanterns

...and I am out with lanterns looking for myself.   Emily Dickinson

Earth seen from space at night
is splattered with light-neurons,
as if impacted by star-falls.

Just a century ago the darkness
would prevail, skyglow would not
block out starlight.

Lanterns gave way to streetlights,
headlights bubbling cities in light--
harsh bulbs in dark places.

Light from malls, stadiums, homes,
buildings, billboards, neon signs--
luminous, attention grabbers shine.

Our energy grid is vulnerable to glitches,
solar flare black-outs–
back to natural light.

When we grow up not seeing stars,
do we disconnect with the cosmos
unlike our star-gazing ancestors?

We are safer and healthier if we reduce
light pollution, staring less at electronic screens
after dark and see our starry galaxy.

I do not have small, hand-held
light sources, only occasional flashlights
to negotiate darkled spaces.

I prefer to look–low tech
with a flickering paper-lantern
to find myself in this high-tech world.

Just Beneath

Just Beneath Anger

Just beneath anger is fear
fear of hurt and loss
loss of control over events
events that are painful to witness
witness of chaos and violence
violence to body and spirit
spirit of love being quenched
quenched by darkness
darkness of ignorance, emptiness
emptiness of light
light necessary for what is just.

Just beneath a leaf
on the windshield, air playfully
brings another flight.

Release

Just
beneath
autumn leaf
wind wriggles stem
free.

Just
beneath
crescent moon
light's sideway smile–
us

Just
beneath
dawning sun
sleepy world wakes
fresh

Just
beneath
verdant lawn
abundant worms
thrive.

Explorations

It's
just
beneath
boundaries
we find escape route
to discover the other side.

It's
just
beneath
Earth's surface
future eruptions
disrupt violent destinies.

It's
just'
beneath
our thin skin
body vessels pump blood
to fulfill our life chart's mission.

Non-Ode to Tossed Salad

Just beneath the tossed salad
bacteria lurks,
salmonella breeds disease,
jumbled veggies yearn
to attack stomach
with virus.
YUCK!

Just Beneath Dreams

Just beneath dreams
is lulling and dulling reality.
Dreaming in bright, luring light
in surreal potentiality
leaves darkled present.
No wonder we dream
for relief from our limitation
and belief in hope.

Missing Rainbows

Be a rainbow in someone's cloud.   Maya Angelou

Sparge of sun drops--
dandelions are the brightest
wildlings in the yard.

Like Icarus' blood spots
cherries redden
on bird-hungry branches.

Petals ruffle in wind
grass gets clipped.
layered stone wall still.

Some days hold rainbows
connect sky to earth
maybe two people.

But today despite being sunny
I do not see rainbows
in some loved ones' clouds.

When will rainbows come to them
for I seem unable to foresee even a sunbow?
We are stuck in place as the garden.

When Love Has Died

How to console someone who tried
to love another? Who to confide?
Who is there as a soothing guide
when love has died, when love has died.

What can one do when partner blurts
their love has left in tiny spurts,
didn't notice despite alerts
when someone hurts, when someone hurts.

When you can only see the signs
of loss despite their best designs,
unravels love which intertwines?
At least one pines. At least one pines.

Wounded Turtle

When will I learn
to shut my mouth
until a better time
when mind and ears open
and listener can hear and see?
I'm a turtle with my head out.
My shell cracking open
from growing pain you cause.

Tumultuary

The front door is open to the night.
My husband is not in bed.
He is not in window-sight.
His bike rests in the garage.
The car parked in the driveway.

We do not seem likely alien abductees.
What aging organs do we have they'd want?
Snoring not sleepwalking
are his normal night habits.
I call to him into the cooling darkness.

In backyard, away from streetlights, he responds.
Through the tangle of dangling, CDs fake deer fence,
past one red plastic safety cone, supposedly
deterring critters' path to his backyard bounty,
I find him in pajamas, camera steadied by hiking pole.

Grandpa's on a mission to capture the supermoon.
Our grandson texted: check out the moon
It looks great. The moon is in nearer orbit.
Like the moon, grandson is entering a new phase.
We all become captives of this bright night.

Sonnenizio for the Supermoon Lunar Eclipse
September 27, 2015   Corvallis, Oregon

Most people are unable to write because they are unable to think and they are unable to think because they lack the equipment to fly over the moon.
H.L. Mencken

Moon-inspired poets step outside from critiques to moon
at the supermoon lunar eclipse–first time since 1982--
rare like a blue moon. In lunar eclipse the moon's face
changes from "blood" moon, blocked black to cleared white.
When moonlight shoots moonbeams, flashlight bright,
howling, moon-eyed poets returned to moonlit poetry.

At Griffiths Observatory moon-gazers
listened to Beethoven's "Moonlight Sonata"
but here poets greeted the changing moonscape,
closest, biggest full harvest moon with awed delight.
Moon, Earth, sun line up, celestial treat witnessed worldwide.
Poets moonwalked back to their poems dreaming moonbows.

On a moon-break, we snack on Moonstruck dark chocolate--
moon round as moon-pies, intoxicating as moonshine.

Musing

light-lit leaves on holly
midline stripe of contrail
wind-puffed clouds

spirits lighten and lift
as I look outside myself
my inside sparkles.

Dimmed Light

Seeking Sang Froid

Coolness of mind, calmness, composure

Sitting in my nightgown, staring at blank white page
on the gray-screen computer background,
tears run down my cheeks as I seek sang froid.
Shivering from grief, I try to poke the keys
to express my heaviness.

I should never start the day reading the newspapers.
The news compounds my internal distress.
I need to be careful what Internet sites I visit
until I get a better grip on my emotions.
Ink gets smudged with dampness.

Meditation does not calm my mind
or deep breathing unless trying to sleep.
I want to be alert, try to resolve my turbulence,
which leaks from my eyes, blurs vision.
Glasses, help me see with clarity.

I peck words from my blue-lighted keyboard.
Like blue birds in a clear sky,
can I lift and lighten my mind atmosphere?
A calming breeze could restore hope.
Rain would not cleanse. Only dampen.

Midnight Visitor

Moments before midnight, loud rapping on front door.
An agitated woman peered through door's window glass.
She was someone I had not seen before.
She chose our home to trespass.
        I asked if I knew her, she said "No."
        She said she was freezing with nowhere to go.

An agitated woman peered through door's window glass.
She claimed she was an ex-Marine.
As she struggled in her mind's morass,
my husband woke and joined the scene.
        She added hot flashes with a feverish glance.
        Could we call for help, an ambulance?

She was someone I had not seen before
so we kept the door locked, called 911.
She hugged a small white blanket, repeated once more
she was lost, a cold ex-Marine, alone.
        Briefly she turned and walked away,
        when we said she could not stay.

She chose our home to trespass.
Might have seemed warmer in an airlock.
Might have seen angel collection alas,
as she looked in at twelve o'clock.
        She returned, said her name, still confused
        but she waited for help. Haven we'd refused.

I asked if I knew her, she said "No."
Huddled in airlock she appeared ghostly gray.
I suggested some safe places I know
that could help her find her way.
        At last a policeman asked what she needed.
        She thanked us. "To the hospital" she pleaded.

She said she was freezing with nowhere to go,
while inside I read poetry under covers, up late.
A string of blue lights rims our door to glow
the dark entrance-- to welcome, celebrate.
        Perhaps these lights beckoned her to us.
        We did not take her in. She left without a fuss.

Shining Moments

Caught on a moment of shining... Paulann Petersen

He addresses his high school graduating class,
twice their class president, an honor student,
invited by them to speak.
He wears a daisy lei over his magenta robe,
Long curly locks ring like a halo
under his mortar board and tassel.
He is barefoot.
He would go on to two more graduations.

Four years later his sister
after struggling toward completion
wore a necklace under the same colored robe
Longer, curly hair flowed under her hat.
Proudly she graduated with her class,
wobbling on white high heels.
She had no further graduations.

Three years before his commencement address
their brother wrote "free bird" on his hat.
A year later on a National Student Exchange
he was killed by a truck
while riding his bike to campus
at the University of Alabama.

Moments of shining have afterglows
of varying duration and differing outcomes.
Graduations spark hope
for many shining moments
for loved ones– all stars
wherever they may be.

Our Son's 50th Birthday

For Kip July 25, 2013

His parents want to celebrate this milestone
but he is not here.
He died in 1982 in an accident
in Tuscaloosa, Alabama at 19
while on a student exchange.
I still miss and love him dearly.

If he had lived he might have
been a husband and father,
continued to bring light and joy.
I've seen him in dreams
but he is young before such commitments.

I have learned not to ask why.
All my excursions into spirituality
provide possibilities and questions.
Do we each have a certain amount of time
to serve in the Earth School
and when our life chart is complete
we can leave at any time.?
Perhaps there are no accidents
and only limited free will.

His death inspires my quest
to understand the universe
not just Earth incarnation.
In a journal of one-sided conversations
as I explained my grief to him.
I freed him to the stars
did not want him to be stuck
to my grief, but to move on.

While undergoing an activation,
the healer said she received
a protocol from Kip from Aldebaran
sending energy to his mother.
Psychics see him as a powerful light being
dashing across the universe.
Some day perhaps our energies
will combine in another form
in another place with light and love.

Rising Softness

Trying to conceal the rising softness
I feel for my younger brother
struggling bravely with stage 4 cancer.
I am trying to appear strong,
supportive through his cancery ordeal.

Over the phone I attempt to console
him with humor and appeal
to our family inheritance of courage.
He is a proud mentor for Livestrong.
He named himself Rickstrong.

He is a computer whiz
who taps into his strengths
to help others prevail.
He uses his writing, music
and animation skills, guides exercise.

A National Autocross champ,
creator of tool design patents,
his edges have rounded
and softened to touch.
He no longer hides his soft sides
but hardens his resolve
to bring hope to others.

Over the phone my softness
reaches out to his.
We are both wired for recovery.

Two Brothers

For Bob and Rick Varsell

My two brothers and I sit on the running board
of our blue Plymouth. I sit next to Rick
who was Ricky then. I am about eight
in a brownie dress, beanie and coat.
Ricky is about three clutching a toy black Scottie
a forerunner of many future dog pets.
Next to Rick is Bob, about thirteen in
a sweatshirt and shorts already into sports.

We three received replicas
of the black and white photo
when Bob turned 80 the day before
I turned 75 at a family smorgasbord party.
We are the last of the full-blooded Swedes
in our Swedish-American family.

Bob became an electrical engineer
with a career working with gyros.
A devoted family man, avid golfer
and reader, funny and satirical,
he wrote two poetry chapbooks
in sibling rivalry with me. Now prefers Sudoku.

Rick became a tool designer
with many patents, a national champion
in auto-cross. He wrote an autobiography.
He created The Whimsical Network on You-Tube,
animating PowerPoint with his own
cartoons, composing music--singing and synthesizer.

The birthday party may be the last time
I see them since I live on the opposite coast.
Both are gravely ill, "cancery" as Rick says.
Both had recent blood clots. Bob's diagnosis
is new, Rick's seven years along.
Rick has been a LiveStrong mentor.
Now they mentor each other
as they face limited options,.
side by side like on the running board,
staring straight ahead
into the unknown.

Changing Expectations

*As life becomes harder and more threatening it also becomes richer, because the
fewer expectations we have, the more good things of life become unexpected gifts
that we accept with gratitude.*   Etty Hillesum

When I flew East in March to celebrate family birthdays
I did not realize it would be the last time I'd see my brothers.
Both brothers died of cancer in May within seventeen days.
It was a shock to me and many others.
> I'd planned to bring them my new book.
> They never had the chance to look.

I did not realize it would be the last time I'd see my brothers
Rick, 69 had breast-lung cancer for seven years.
Bob, 80 had undiagnosed bladder bothers.
Both were running out of time it appears.
> The Swedish smorgasbord party filled with joy
> would be the last we three Swedes would enjoy.

Both brothers died of cancer in May within seventeen days.
My own maladies kept me from flying back.
I was trying healing in untraditional ways,
not getting any additional feedback.
> I had to learn not to expect too much,
> even when I needed a strong crutch.

It was a shock to me and many others.
It was time to help their families cope.
Time to listen to the children and mothers,
Time to offer comfort and hope.
> We all drew closer from these losses
> trying to toss our albatrosses.

I'd planned to bring them my new book.
We shared creative projects and cheered
siblings across continent to brook
distance until contact disappeared.
> When at last the book was finished,
> I felt part of my happiness diminished.

They never had the chance to look
but others did and lifted my heart.
While I was grieving, readers took
time to support and played their part
> to uplift my sagging soul,
> healing pieces to make me whole.

Resilience

Let laughter call you from your cave. Join activists you admire.
Leap more, dance more– Smile more, laugh more.
Gravity is a habit that is hard to break.
                Carolyn Myers

As I grieve the deaths of my only two brothers
in the same month of May, 17 days apart
I know I must cope as I have with other losses
offering support to loved ones and begin
the return to the people and passions
which make me more alive and giving.

For me it will mean reaching out
to family and friends, poetry,
causes I am dedicated to, teaching, learning.
But right now my tamped spirit
struggles for words to express
what I am feeling. My body is heavy.

Pundits suggest we receive our greatest lessons
in our darkest times, wallowing until we see light.
Not my preferred way to fulfill my quests.
Pain of any kind wounds deeply.
Gravity may tug, but I will laugh and leap,
dance, word-play, share light again–somehow.

Healing Song

Many leaps must happen
from ego to pain to singing.
Not so hard for an ego
to experience pain
but to jump to singing–
that is the hard part.

Following the sequence to some order
from chaos, might require a conductor
toward singing. A solo needs a score,
practice in reading the music.

When eyes are blurry with tears
it is hard to see a way out of pain.
Music usually requires an instrument to perform.
Singing needs a clear voice.

An ego engulfed in pain seeks solace.
Some find it in singing.
The Earth has a song which people muffle.
Pain has a rhythm- out of step.
We seek the right tone.

I listen to singing when in pain.
I am not soothed by my raspy song.
Some music is dissonant.
If pain is to lead to singing,
I need lessons, a good ear,
relief from non-resonating strings.
Sometimes a brief surcease,
a surge of joy–rarely singing
releases pain. I relax, laugh
and write about it.

Room for Forgotten Souls
                1914-1971

Ashes in 3,447 copper urns
of forgotten souls from mental institutions
many unclaimed by relatives, some unidentified
have been found and remembered.

Stacked in a crematorium, floor to ceiling
in the decrepit Oregon State Hospital
of One Flew Over the Cuckoo's Nest fame
corroded urns, part of the dark past of this place.

A new facility contains a memorial metal wall
with new ceramic urns transferred from copper canisters
to protect patients in death, like they were rarely
cared for in life.–a reminder of our painful mistreatment.

Urns embedded in the wall are engraved
with patients' names, urn number, life span.
If they are claimed , the nameplate is removed.
Only 183 were claimed.

Native Americans are returned to their tribes
for their own ceremonies. Some remains received a military burial.
Scant records reveal stunted lives from various conditions
new treatments and facilities could have helped.

Patients came from 48 states, born in 44 countries.
At least 110 veterans–some dishonorably discharged.
await family members who might not know they are there
who can search on-line data bases.

Souls from most common states: Oregon, Illinois, Iowa
born from most common countries: Sweden, Germany, Finland
A delusional saddler from Bohemia, a wandering Norwegian laborer,
a pilfering woman ejected from a nursing home.

The wall also honors 1,566 missing bodies
who disappeared from the old hospital cemetery.
Visitors peer into a hollow void.
These bodies are still lost.

Some patients suffered from depression, delusions, bi-polar,
physical and developmental disabilities, some were left
because families did not know what to do with them,
not knowing what would happen to them in this dark place.

Many souls have names etched on tombstones,
military memorial walls, some cremains were scattered.
People pass on, unremembered, unrecorded
joining these forgotten souls stuck in a wall.

Mustering the Light

I imagine the lure in utter dark. I play it lightly. Peter Sears

The gyres of grief lure utter darkness.
You spiral from the sense of loss.
Thoughts blur. Light feels as distant as stars.

As you heal you can turn
from wallowing in grief
to honor the light your loved ones brought.

You can choose to share whatever light
you can muster to lighten others,
until darkness is less heavy.

Despite enticement of self pity,
I chose to play life lightly.
to cope and celebrate beloveds.

Each word, each action
a reaction against fear toward love.
so pain has a purpose for light.

Shifting Light

I have been resting
listening to a CD where angels
remove darkness from my soul
for all possible lives...hopefully.

I have tried all kind of games
to try to heal my wounds
to body, mind and spirit. My soul
still struggles to break free.

This Earth life is apparently
one of many past and future lives,
simultaneous and all happening now
as there is no time. Beyond my scope.

I have tried prayer, meditation, a talisman
Western doctors, a shaman, Health Detective,
acupuncture, massage, knee bands, heat, cold,
Quantum Healing Hypnotic Therapy.

I have consulted books in many fields, videos,
intuitive consultants, counselors, used magnetic coils.
water and physical therapy, exercise,
diet, herbs, medications and creams.

I understand we make ourselves sick
and can make ourselves well.
So far I have not healed
and I need more interventions.

My maladies could come from challenges
I placed in my life chart before birth.
They might be leftovers from other lives.
Whatever the source they are painful.

If I am to be a light-bringer,
fulfill my mission successfully,
could perform better, emit more positively,
if light could flow through me clearer.

I want my energies to flourish,
aura bright (I kind of like blue),
cooperating, repairing, exuding,
            If only like a contrail
                        pain could dissipate.

Seasonal Light

Sky-Watcher

Contrails rip and rend the air.
Fogdogs peek through fog banks.
Clouds sculpt and shift.

I watch the sky fly by.
The window frames each change.
I witness an aerial merry-go-round.

Tints and shades of light
tell me what time it is and what
weather conditions I'm sheltered from.

Pollution must be churning.
Satellites orbit.
Sun, moon, stellar objects glow.

Comfy on the couch
my celestial screen
entertains and insights wonder.

Changing the Guard

Writing amid seasonal decorations

Time to change holiday decorations
I am changing the Valentine guards
from tables and bathroom congregations.
Now spring and Easter inspire bards.
As we write first drafts in perspiration
we have perky creatures for inspiration.

I am changing the Valentine guards
with cupids and red-dressed creatures.
Hearts and arrows are discards
as I put up springy, flowery features.
Of course some Christmas lurks in crannies--
lingering favorites of this granny's.

From tables and bathroom, congregations
go into the closet, into hiding.
Boxed away to their hibernations
they await their seasonal awakenings. Guiding
their rest, I touch each gently with joy
until all packed away, ready to deploy.

Now spring and Easter inspire bards
our writing will magically take flight.
Time to claim our desired rewards
as we create with amiable delight.
We write with bunnies, ducks and chicks,
any approach if brings word clicks.

As we write first drafts in perspiration
silently our writing group's on task.
Despite our inner desperation,
we carry on and do not ask
if any of this decor is our muse.
They exude light we can't refuse.

We have perky creatures for inspiration
when mind's drained and hand's still.
We re-focus on our new creation
let down our guard, to refill.
The ambiance of color in the room
brings light to dispel any gloom.

Spring Haiku

parking lot drains rain
river of oily rainbow
through grate

wind tickles wind chimes
giggles in brisk breeze
rarely silent

black cells at Hanford
leak toward Columbia
river cancer

men in white lace
blood-red capes
suppress women's voices

fresh-cut yellow daffodil
propped against windshield
planted by stranger

cherry blossoms
blush in fog waiting
to shine

Easter Bunny
populates new recruits
eagerly   yearly

Let Go

Through my car's windshield I watch
as a stripping sapling lets go of its leaves,
silhouetted against gray sky, a shadow play.
Leaves like a bat, birds, cat waggling its tail.
The windstorm shivers and quivers remnants
clinging to spindly branches,
hugging near the narrow trunk.

Most leaves quake and shake
rock and roll with gusto,
but one acrobatic leaf
spins like a helicopter
swirls and twirls beside a smaller leaf.
At times the two appear to connect like butterfly wings.

This one leaf cannot still,
blowing with each blast without rest,
narrow stem to thin offshoot.
Rain speckles the windshield,
pelts the leaf, moistens it
over the adjoining leaf,
plasters them together,
bandages them to the branch
glistening with rain.

Soggily they await the storm's passing.
At the right time, they will let go
after their momentary respite.

Witches Chant

I'm coming to get you
for my Halloween stew.
My cauldron is boiling–
just waiting for you.

I'm coming to get you.
You have such succulent fat.
You'll make my brew tasty.
Can't beat belly bulge–drat!

I'm coming to get you
but you are outside my snare.
You are full of dark chocolate.
Of your sweet tooth, I'm aware.

I'm coming to get you.
Your diet Coke will add some fizz.
That lamb chops' digesting–yum.
I can't grab you. Gee whizz.

I'm coming to get you
for your bubbly, brothy, gelatinous ingredients
are just what I need. Come on go outside,
indulge my disobedience.

I'm coming to get you.
Just step outside your car
and I will snatch you
wherever you are.

I'm coming to get you!
I'll come right to your door.
I'll be a trick-or-treater
and I'll grab you– before....

I'll take you to my coven
prepare you for our feast.
But you are heavy–so cooperate.
Jump in the cauldron at least.

You like warm water
and when we are through
you'll be a delicious gourmet treat.
I'm coming to get you.

Grumpy Pumpkin

Lit
pumpkin
dim, grimaced
jack-o-lantern,
gap-toothed, growing fuzz
beginning to shrivel,
harvested too soon to cut.
Saggy, soggy pumpkin head, so
droopy, candlelight squeaks through bleakly.
Did your smile become a frown by Halloween?

Holiday Crunches

Halloween, Thanksgiving, Christmas crunch
into a hectic, too short, festive bunch.
Witches turn to Pilgrims, Indians to Santa Claus,
Cats and bats to turkeys then reindeer paws.

Jack-o-lanterns to cornucopias to Christmas star
trick or treat to pumpkin pie to gifts from afar.
Traditions vary for each celebration
with rituals and their changes in ration.

If you decorate with holiday creatures
you'll notice how they morph features
to certain animals or fantasy beings
depending on what you're used to seeing.

Between Valentine's Day and Easter–some breather
May Day to Fourth of July not crowded either.
But fall or early winter holidays clump.
It is hard to lighten a heavy lump.

But candy and other seasonal sweets
seem constant for celebratory treats.
The trends seems scaring to sharing.
The intention is bearing to caring.

You just have to want to celebrate
whether you are on time or late.
Find some way for a fun occasion
and you won't need much persuasion.

Putting Up Christmas Decorations

When I put up Christmas decorations
I have to plan to do it in stages
Each year I make modifications
as the display and decorator ages.
So many miniatures were my mother's
and the creativity of many others.

I have to plan to do it in stages
The displays can take days to complete.
With few directions and adages
on how to design and not repeat.
As figures emerge from boxes I see
just where I want their essence to be.

Each year I make modifications
Arrangements tend to shift places.
Of course I must absorb additions,
so new forms find their spaces.
Color and texture brighten day and night
to make the winter season bright.

As the display and decorator ages
I leave up decorations for months or more
While some areas have seasonal collages,
other remain with Christmas decor.
Beloved creatures seem alive, become
a treasured companion in our home.

So many miniatures were my mother's
Many are from Swedish folk art collections.
Painted wooden ornaments from her and brothers
bring back many childhood recollections.
I survey my delightful queendom
and shout to all a heartfelt welcome.

And the creativity of many others
brings me happy holiday delight.
And if I had my druthers
I would still unfurl their light.
Though weary I will persevere
and joyfully set them up this year.

Christmas Procrastination Ritual

We must decorate our house today!
Have not gotten very far.
Take boxes from shelves! To cheer ourselves
we'll sneak cookies from the cookie jar.

But Christmas is just two weeks away.
Such lollygags we all are!
To cheer ourselves, take boxes from shelves.
We will first need a chocolate bar.

We will try anything to delay,
but can't stop the calendar.
Take boxes from shelves to cheer ourselves–
time for love, light, to dream on a star.

Winter Solstice

On this winter solstice yearning for light
I ponder my purpose for being here.
Striving for meaning, direction, delight
in this season of love, peace, good cheer.
What have I learned in this Earth School
I can share on this upcoming Yule?

I ponder my purpose for being here,
whether what we do actually matters.
Is my cosmic consciousness connection clear?
Can I stay on track when a dream shatters?
Will I be forthright and brave
facing obstacles...or cave?

Striving for meaning, direction, delight
my meandering path strolls toward soul.
Hopes flicker like candlelight,
as I wander toward my life's goal.
Head and heart lead my way
toward gratitude this holiday.

In this season of love, peace, good cheer
I find I must prepare.
Creating joy it would appear
is a gift we can share.
When I search within for meaning,
it is soul awareness I'm gleaning.

What have I learned in this Earth School?
Life presents light and dark chances.
Can we control the unkind and cruel?
Sometimes choice is what enhances
the possibility of resolution
and the opportunity for evolution.

I can share on this upcoming Yule.
I believe the universe can support us.
We may stray from the Golden Rule
but angels might not report us.
With gratefulness, hope and trust
I'll roll a dust bunny with my star dust.

Triolet Trio for Secular Christmas

Christmas Eve

Will angels sing for us tonight?
    We listen down below,
with candlelight beneath starlight.
Will angels sing for us tonight?
Through windows peering into night
    follow light, want to know
will angels sing for us tonight?
    We listen down below.

Christmas Day

Light the candles. Sing festive song.
    No matter if believe.
It's season to feel all belong.
Light the candles. Sing festive song.
Celebrate loving all daylong,
    not wanting light to leave.
Light the candles. Sing festive song.
    No matter if believe.

Day After Christmas

Be grateful for all your gifts,
    even some you don't like.
Enjoy the intent, spirit lifts.
Be grateful for all your gifts.
Remember as memory drifts
    love shared to all alike.
Be grateful for all of your gifts
    even some you don't like.

Winter Lights

Lights around the winter solstice
gleam through penetrating dark.
Time for host and hostess

to celebrate festivals of lights.
Belief traditions around the world–
enlightening, bringing delight.

Time for harmony and justice.
Time for a peaceful spark.
Lights around the winter solstice

beckon, welcome, make lives bright.
Switch on bulbs. Light candles.
Belief traditions around the world

flicker, glimmer under starlight,
use words like twas, lo and hark.
Time for host and hostess

feasting, gifting. Faith handles
expressions of connection and joy.
Switch on bulbs. Light candles.

Shine with warmth to entice
holidays spirits, kind remark.
Light around the winter solstice

lift season's promise, help you enjoy
dreams of a lighter place,
expressions of connection and joy.

A good intention will suffice.
Smile–think of rainbow's arc.
Time for host and hostess

to greet guests with hospitality, grace.
Time for beloveds to gather
dreams of a lighter place.

Time for gratitude is good advice.
Find a space where love can park.
Lights around the winter solstice,
time for host and hostess.

Join in, (Wouldn't you rather?)
to celebrate festivals of light.
Time for beloveds to gather
enlightening, bringing delight.

Light a Candle for Winter Festivals of Light.

1. Light a candle for Diwali, the Hindu Festival of Lights.
    Add feasting, dancing, parades, fireworks exploding light.

2. Light a candle for Ashura, the Sunni and Jewish celebration
    of Yom Kippur with the Day of Atonement.

3. Light a candle for Feast of St. Nicholas
    a Dutch tradition that may have inspired Santa Claus.

4. Light a candle for Bodhi Day for Buddhists
    who celebrate Buddha's enlightenment.

5. Light a candle for Catholic's Feast of Immaculate Conception
    to honor Mary who they believe was born without sin.

6. Light a candle for Catholics' feast of our Lady of Guadalupe.
    Hispanic Catholics celebrate an apparition.

7. Light a candle for St. Lucia Day, the beginning of God Jul
    who wears a crown of lighted candles like a halo around her head.

8. Light a candle for the Mexican Posadas
    whose processions have candles, electric lights and fireworks.

9. Light a candle for Jewish festival of Chanukah
    who light 8 candles on a candelabra.

10. Light a candle for Yalda, a Persian celebration of the winter solstice.
    Mithra, was a Persian angel of light and truth.

11. Light a candle for Saturnalia. a Roman winter solstice celebration
    a celebration of personal freedom.

12. Light a candle for Yule or winter solstice or Yule
    a festival for Wiccans and Pagans.

13. Light a candle for Christmas with lights in the windows,
    in processions and dazzling on the Christmas trees.

14. Light a candle for the ancient Egyptian and Syrian celebration
    of the sun as an infant at the winter solstice.

15. Light a candle for the Zoroastrians' celebration of Zarathustra
    who had the idea of one eternal God and seven powerful creations.

16. Light a candle of Kwanza, the African-American celebration of unity, self-determination, collective work and responsibility, creativity faith.

17. Light a candle for the Buddhist Sculpture Festival- Buddhist New Year Buddhist monks create yak butter sculptures lit with special butter lamps.

18. Light a candle for Chaomos, the Pakistan Winter Solstice celebrated with purification rituals, singing, dancing, feasting on goat tripe and bonfires.

19. Light a candle for Dosmoche, the Tibetan Celebration of the Dying Year with a magical pole covered with stars, crosses, pentagrams made of string.

20. Light a candle for El Dia de Los Tres Reyes- Three Kings Day celebrating the Three Kings also called Epiphany. Place straw for the camels on beds.

21. Light a candle for the Feast of the Ass from the Middle ages-a parody with an ass lead into the church and the congregation brayed like asses.

22. Light a candle for Ganna, the Ethiopian Christmas. Shepherds waved hooked staffs at Christ's birth and they devised the game called Ganna played January 7th.

23. Light a candle for Hari-Kuyo the Japanese Festival of the Broken Needles For all who sew- a shrine made for needles with offerings of food, scissors, thimbles.

24. Light a candle for La Befana- Italy's Santa Claus, a kindly witch with toys who leaves gifts for children while looking for the "holy child" in each household.

25. Light a candle for Midvinterblot, a winter solstice Swedish celebration "mid-winter-blood" formerly featuring animal and human sacrifice in pagan times.

26. Light a candle for the Night of the Radishes- in Oaxaca, Mexico. Artisans carve radishes into Biblical and Aztec legend scenes.

27. Light a candle to Northern European Pagan Celebrations on Winter Solstice. Called Yule with Yule log, singing and dancing around fire to awaken sun.

28. Light a candle for Sacaea, a Babylonian winter observance which features ritually killing the king to secure continuity and renewal with jollity and celebration.

29. Light a candle for the Snap Dragon Christmas game from England. Set brandy in a bowl on fire, throw raisins in, snap flaming raisins to your mouth.

30. Light a candle for Wassailing the Apple Trees on Twelfth night in England. Men fire at apple tree. drink cider, party guessing the roast prepared, make merry.

31. Light a candle for the Winter Solstice generally on December 21th Daylight is shortest and nights are the longest at this time of year

32. Light a candle for Zagmuk the oldest winter festival recorded in Mesopotamia. celebrating god Marduk's victory over darkness and chaos.

33. Light a candle for the Buddhist festival of lights Tazaungdine Festival in Burma. Hot air balloons lit with candles released to celebrate full moon day and almsgiving.

34. Light a candle for French Christmas traditions of Light with advent candles lit four consecutive Sundays before Christmas day and a Yule log.

35. Light a candle for St, Martin's Day, a festival of light from Holland where children carry lanterns, get candy and treats when singing house to house.

36. Light a candle for Loi Krathong festival of light in Thailand. They float a lotus-shaped vessel of banana leaves holding a candle, joss-sticks, flowers, coins.

37. Light a candle for Egyptian Christmas of the Coptic Orthodox Church. Copts give candles to the poor, decorate with lights, 7 gifts exchanged, buy new clothes.

38. Light a candle for Christmas in the Philippines with "parols" or star lanterns. Parols in homes and in processions as well as fireworks.

39. Light a candle for Christmas in China where Christmas trees are called "trees of light" with paper chains, flowers and lanterns.

40. Light a candle for Christmas in Mexico. They march with candles house to house looking for room at the inn. They celebrate with pinatas, put out shoes for gifts.

41. Light a candle for New Year's Eve in Brazil where they ask Iemanja, African goddess of waters to give them good luck by putting candles in the sand.

Mistaken Identities

-1- Festivals of Light

Celebrations of winterlight decorations usually come down in April.
Festivals of Light: creches, Kwanzaa candles, menorahs,
Swedish candlesticks, Star Boys and Lucia with candle crowns
boxed and stored for another season.

Our grandson brings trays full of Swedish miniature
Star Boys and Lucias for me to wrap.
Blonde Lucias wear wreaths on their heads
holding candles–white as a winter moon.
Her snow white gown ties with a red sash at the waist.

Star Boys in milky gowns, vanilla, pointed, cone-shaped hats
splattered with golden stars. One star tops his staff.

Our grandson places the last tray load on the table.
He asks, "Grandma, why do you collect the Ku Klux Klan?

How can he think his equal rights advocate, feminist,
liberal Democrat, dovish-Aries grandmother
would consider collecting the KKK whose only similarity
to Lucias and Star Boys is wearing white gowns?

-2- Hybrid Identity

His grandmother is the last generation full-blooded
Swedish-American in our family.
Lucia and Star Boy also acquired a hybrid identity.

Italian Lucia was a beautiful Christian girl of a wealthy family
in the 3rd century. A devoted daughter who prayed her ill mother
to a miraculous recovery and decided to live a virgin,
gave away her dowry and all her belongings.
Her fiancé brought her to court and accused her of being a Christian.

Heart-broken Lucia poked a needle in her eyes to blind herself.
But despite destroyed eyes, she could see.
She is portrayed holding two eyeballs on a tray.

A judge ordered her to leave Syracuse but she refused.
1000 men, oxen and trolls could not move her.
They covered her with tar and set her on fire.

Neither Lucia nor her red dress were harmed.
Her former fiancé stabbed her neck with a sword
which killed her on December 13th 304 AD.
The Catholic church proclaimed her a saint.
They say she is buried in Venice in the red death dress.

Star Boy also has saintly origins.
Stephanos told King Herod the King of the Jews was born.
Herod said it was as likely as if a fried rooster
came alive and called. The rooster flew and called:
"Christus natus est." Christ is born.
Herod ordered Stephanus punished.
One version says he was stoned.
Another legend says they poked his eyes out
but like Lucia he could see. Eyeballs like chicken eggs.
Either way, he became a saint.

-3- Swedish Lucia and Star Boy

Lucia means light. In snowbound, sun-starved Sweden
Lucia's death date December 13th was considered the longest night.
When Sweden became Catholic, Lucia became a symbol of light.
They conceived her shining like an angel–radiant halo or even wings.

This long night conjured ghosts and spirits coming to life.
Animals talking. Best not to go out. But if you do,
some dressed in scary and funny costumes.
Males dressed as brides.
They rose early and ate three breakfasts
of coffee, Lucia cats or saffron buns and gingerbread.

When Sweden became Lutherans, they kept Lucia traditions.
Lucia still wears a sheet-white gown, sash red as a sword slash,
a crown of greens (often lingonberry leaves) with five to nine candles.
Today children often wear battery-powered lights in the crown.

Modern Lucias visit Syracuse as part of their annual religious procession
to do charity work and collect money for the poor around the world.
On Lucia Day-December 13th Swedish children as Lucia and Star Boys carry a tray
to serve parents breakfast in bed: coffee, lussekatter and gingerbread.
This also takes place in schools, hospitals, companies–almost everywhere.

-4- My White Gowns

My grandson would not think of my white gowns.
I do not remember playing Lucia to my Swedish-American parents.

No white graduation gown. No white choir robe-just stiff white collar.
In several Christmas pageants I played angels in unblemished white gowns
and wings. My long blonde hair resembled Lucia.

My white gown began with a diaper-white Christening dress.
My cloud-nine white prom dress sprinkled with blue roses had a blue sash.
A New England teen not a Southern Belle decked in white
walking to the prom on the arm of a sheltering father.
In fiction lily-white costumes for the heroine's
innocence, purity, honesty and simplicity.

My virginal white-laced bridal gown over pure-white underskirts
has been boxed since being married over fifty years ago
by Congregational Reverend Sterling White.

-5- Angel Collector

My grandson would not confuse Lucia and Star Boys for angels.
Thousands of angels flitter from ceilings, litter surfaces,
symbols of creativity and uplifting spirits
serving as muses for the writers who create among them.

My grandson would not suspect the other winged-ones
in my mini-museum–earth-toned fairies, elves and owls.
It is comforting to be surrounded by light-beings.

-6- Poet's White Dress

My grandson would not make the metaphorical leap
to the white dresses of Emily Dickinson.
She began wearing all-white after her father's death
for controversial reasons only she knew for sure
but others felt free to speculate upon.
She was buried in one of her paper-white dresses.

-7- Grandpa's No Star Boy

Non-Swedish grandpa never played the role of the Star Boy,
but he was an Episcopalian altar boy in a habit–
black gown, a white top with poofy sleeves,
sometimes a server, sometimes carrying a cross.

But as a cultural anthropology professor,
a white gown might suggest an Arab's thobe
or dishdasha and turban.

-8- Light Trinity

Our grandson with his lapsed Catholic/Protestant heritage
is not familiar with spiritual white garb like clerical robes,
white nuns, missionary fathers–white men in white gowns
neck to wrists and ankles, or a Pope.
He might not have seen white communion dresses.

He is more likely to think wearing white as tennis or military whites,
nurses and doctors serving others in uniforms
white as bandages, bones, leukemia cells, cotton balls, aspirin.

-9- Dark Trinity

Our grandson probably heard of the Klan in history class
part of the civil rights struggle perhaps.
White Supremacists, believers in an Aryan nation–
white with fury, white flames, marbled positions, ashen, pallid countenance,
to white-wash, white-out others,
watching chalky segregation rubbing away.

Black magic not white magic.
White pieces in a chess game pouncing to checkmate black pieces.
Their ritual book the Kloran.

Cloaked in fear and hatred, the Klan's white costume derived from Spain.
Spanish holy week–in act of penance for unholy deeds–
they wore white clothes and conical hats called capirotes, like a dunce cap.

The Klan wears white costumes, robes, masks, conical hats
to conceal their identity. Eye-slots through white fabric.
Klan's alabaster robes can be found on the Internet
with cape, belt, patch, hard-liner accessories
on 50/50 cotton polyester called politically incorrect,
bizarre conversation pieces, unusual Halloween costumes or collector's items.

-10- Name the Light

Our grandson's surname LeClair means "the light".
His mother and uncle served his grandparents
as Lucia and Star Boy as children. He has not done so.
But he has Italian/French/Northern European ancestry.

After explaining the light ties and symbolism
of Lucia and Star Boy traditions, he suggests–
"Why not collect the Kookamunga Cracker Killers?"
"Who are they, " asks his bewildered grandma.
"I don't know, I made them up."
I guess he is making me up as well.
Do we all make up our identities?

I was as puzzled as some Nobel Prize winners who were surprised
with a singing Lucia procession early in the morning
while they're still in bed at their hotel.

I hope my grandson can perceive me in a whiter light.
To me he is a shining Star Boy.

-11- Light-Bringers

White contains all the colors of the spectrum.
With pasty, pale Nordic skin and whitening hair, I'd blanch
if I wore a whipped-cream-white gown. I'd look like a ghost- a white shadow.
I tend to wear blue and pants.
Once I was blonde and still blue-eyed--
the colors of the Swedish flag.

But I am an American, I aspire to be a modern Lucia–
a light-bearer who dances poetic leaps in a rainbow culotte costume,
whose wreath of recycled artificial greens has flashlight pens poking out,
who carries a serving tray like a blank page at my fingertips
who wants to side with the light to make a better world,
who hopes to transit like a white butterfly
to the white light at the end of the tunnel
to a whitened realm of whitening lives,
hula-hooping halos.

Sea-foamed haired Grandpa, my star-studded Star Boy
wearing a flat cap, walking with a birch hiking stick,
my trusted assistant can jog along.

Our identities are often misunderstood and mis-perceived.
I will never view Lucias and Star Boys quite the same way.
Like my grandson discovered, white gowns are open to
interpretation.

Contemplating Light

Trying to See the Light

In my cosmic journey through space/time
I wonder if this time I was delivered
to the wrong womb at the wrong time
on the wrong planet.

Because after decades of studying
the purpose of life on Earth
for all of its inhabitants
I still don't seem to fully see the light.

A 3D dualistic reality is not very harmonious,
a tug of war of difference
not the light-full ALL-ness connectedness
to the Prime Creator I would hope for.

One theory is this Curious Prime Creator
sent out parts of its essence--
energized souls to splatter the multiverse
to experience life and report back.

This source of light allowed darkness
to see how souls can cope with it.
Why was this necessary? The sky
is filled with darkness just spots of light.

Another theory says this God is loving,
anthropomorphized into parents
at least for Earthlings to understand.
Can't beings learn love without suffering?

An all-knowing God should not need
all these data collectors. Creativity
is more important than knowledge, so
maybe Prime Creator needed mini-creators' dreams.

The ground rules on Earth supposedly
started out as a Utopian experiment,
but dark entities fought with light ones
and we are the spoils. The light lost.

If we do indeed have free will and come from light
why would we want to bleep out? Darkle?
The Prime Creator vicariously experiences
what under limiting conditions we create.

Some pretty eternally impossible standards
required to reunite with the Source of Light.
Many cosmic casualties en route.
Can we ever experience enough to graduate?

My research indicates that I am
a Pleiadean Blue Ray attached
to the Divine Feminine and I chose
to help the evolution of the human race.

I scoured the Internet and books
as to what duties I took on.
I passed the test for a Starseed.
It is as out there a theory as just living here.

I need to develop the attitude
and aptitude to be of assistance
if indeed 3D Earth gives us the heave-ho
and we need to ascend to 5D Earth...or elsewhere.

In such a mind-boggling big multiverse
there must be other sentient options beyond
what this DNA tweaked body can contemplate.
Are we all an ort of some divine dreamer?

I am not sure exactly what divine means
in a cosmic context. Earthly suggestions
appear too divisive, based on fear,
tend to lead to violence not love.

So though I am unsure about why I came,
in a more multiversal context I might know.
Perhaps I am a renegade and ambassador to release fear,
since I'm attracted to love, light and harmony.

I'd like to be a systems buster, alter codes
and consciousness, be free to evolve
from the dark side's negative restrictions,
help raise the frequency of us all.

I do not want to experience
what humans have done to each other
or the Earth, unless positive change
is possible for all of creation.

Creating a Cosmic Perspective

`Religion is politics in the sky. Gloria Steinem

Religion has the same mostly male hierarchy as politics.
Various interpretations of the love/God theme
leads to violence, female suppression, wars.
Some "He" is in charge of human affairs.

The term spirituality is more inclusive.
The energy distributer, Prime Creator is in everything.
We are all linked in a circle, not climbing
a pyramid pointing upward with many at the bottom.

The Buddhists seem more philosophical and grounded,
concerned with right concentration, mindfulness,
effort, livelihood, action, speech, intention and view.
Right does not appear extremist here.

They don't believe they are tethered to an eternal soul
and leave their deceased body to replenish the earth.
They do not seem to engage in many fabrications.
No theocracies to kill or die for. Fewer wars for Buddha.

Buddhism does not require belief or worship
of a supernatural creator, personal God,
no unconditional faith in truths and dogmas.
Perhaps the most open minded group with no God.

Buddha tried to transform suffering.
We suffer due to ignorance, negative emotions,
pursue illusions, are closed-minded, self-focused.
Buddha teaches impermanence, interconnectedness.

Science also theorizes all life forms are interconnected.
Buddhists believe we are part of a commonwealth of beings.
They try to live harmoniously and nonviolently with compassion.
Know oneself. Avoid excesses. It is a kind path to happiness.

I'm evolving a cosmic perspective. Perhaps we are soul-facets,
spewed from a Prime Creator to experience and create many lives.
Maybe we are part of ALL in an infinite diverse multiverse.
I believe in light, love, compassionate connectedness.

I am collecting bits of light from many perspectives
to create my own mirrored disco ball for my cosmic dances.
My internal authentic power looks at external powers.
Hopefully my free will can shirk the controllers. I am open to a better way.

Why Am I Here?

Is my soul
part of a whole
in this Earth role

or good sport
as an ort
of some sort ?

Do I come from
some star slum,
some star chum?

Why am I here?
Is it too cheer
with ones dear?

Am I a spark
of light in the dark
to leave my mark?

Blue Light

During a past life regression session
the shaman saw me enveloped in blue light.
I could only see blue-tinted eyelids.

Entrancing words tried to lure me into trance,
but I could not go where bidden, remained
stuck in the present with my blue eye-patches.

The shaman sensed in my blue fog a heavy sadness.
From the early 1900s, he saw images
of a woman and child running beside a river.

Thrashing through tall grass edging the water,
I tripped and gashed my knees on rocks.
The child died in an accident. I was devastated.

The shaman said the boy's name was John
and my sadness lingered from that death.
John was the same spirit as my present life son Kip.

In 1982 Kip went on a student exchange
and died in a bike-truck accident
at the age of 19 in Tuscaloosa, Alabama.

Two mothers lost two sons connected by karma.
A psychic said Kip had given me another chance
to experience tragedy without crumbling as before.

An intuitive told me Kip's death
was a sacrifice so I'd evolve spiritually–
a burden of guilt I'd carried for decades.

But the shaman heard Kip's adamant protest.
"No Mom, I came in for myself. I love you
for allowing me to live and do what I came to do."

Kip was emphatic. I had it all wrong.
I gave him the gift of life. He was grateful.
        I felt so much lighter and freed.

I would never want anyone to sacrifice their life
for my advancement. I was deeply troubled to think I did.
        Kip was a gift to all who knew and loved him.

Kip has come to my aid to boost energy before,
but he forgot to mention he lived here for his karma.
        It would have been good to know sooner but–

searching for why he died I did discover
aspects of spirituality and cosmic connections.
        I was told he completed his mission.

I adore my celestial son–now lighting the cosmos.
I have seen him in dreams and apparently
our starships cross paths in other dimensions.

The shaman unveiled past unknowings.
Now I can move onward less encumbered, knowing
        I enabled his destiny. We gifted each other.

The shaman begins to heal my bone-on-bone arthritic knees.
The pain lessens. Someday I may dance again like in some
of my more spritely, dancerly lifetimes...glowing blue.

Family of Light

If it is true as many believe
we choose our life's destiny,
we create what we receive,
we choose our time and family,
         I hope I joined the family of light
         to turn darkness lovingly bright.

We choose our life's destiny
before we enter this destination.
I'm told I came with a little mutiny
but committed to participation.
         Earth needed a wake up call
         and I wanted part in the protocol.

We choose what we receive.
Somewhere in the multiverse
a creator could conceive
a new experiment for this universe.
         Souls splintered to the scene
         to see what this could mean.

We choose our time and family
based on what we need to learn,
or some kind of puzzling anomaly.
A peaceful place is what I yearn.
         In the splendiferous cosmos somewhere
         is a light-ful existence I'd like to share.

I hope I joined the family of light
for all my experiences into being
with growing knowledge and insight
to understand the changes I'm seeing.
         I hope this galactic neighborhood
         is evolving toward greater good.

To turn darkness lovingly bright
from dark energies' destructive force
would bring light-bringers delight
and harmony to ALL of course.
         As long as I dwell in dualistic 3D,
         it's a dream, not my current reality.

Preparing for the Shift

Every jot and tittle of the Law will be fulfilled.   Edgar Cayce

If I am to raise my frequency
to pass through a stargate
to the 5th dimensional New Earth,
I have many hurdles and hoops
to overcome. I need stamina and help.
I want clarity and courage.

I need to tweak my DNA strands,
all my energy bodies, release false beliefs,
work with Spiritual Assistants to boost
my dimensional consciousness, balance
body with holographic template,
to a passable, acceptable range.

I should use the Violet Flame technique
for all body parts to re-pattern, restructure,
rejuvenate all my organs, glands and physical body
to balance energy patterns to obtain a new body.
I should complete the Melchizedek Program
to stop or reverse aging,

align my "light body" through the chakra system,
build a Mer-ka-ba Energy Field, erase
the Master Cell of past-life program encodements,
clear with properly phrased questions
discordant programs and holding patterns,
avoid mycoplasmas pathogens,

strive for love the highest frequency,
call for help from Creator of Love, Creator of Light,
Creator of New Body Parts and Creator of Health,
initiate through Seven Temples of Ascension.
I may have done some of them
in a previous incarnation...or not,

take complete control of the mind and monitor
every thought which effects all of creation,
balance and align consciousness at all levels,
attune mind to soul and heart,
reduce warrior consciousness and negativity,
neutralize any subatomic malfunctioning creations.

control dreams, 4 minds and cosmic minds
in harmony, balanced and integrated into oneness,
discipline minds, emotions, bodies
and all levels of consciousness for proper vibration
for attunement for the soul, avoid bowing down
to the illusion of ego, work with subtle energy,

be enthusiastic when all energy bodies synchronized
and aligned and strongly integrated. (I'd be exhausted),
transmute one form of energy into another,(Energy follows thought.)
balance feminine and masculine aspects of self,
love unconditionally, live with integrity, detach from space/time,
think carefully before I speak, choose words carefully,

learn dowsing techniques to appraise progress,
study Twelve Golden Principles for Ascension.
Understand and apply universal laws
and shifts in consciousness. So many aspects
to activate before Earth cleanses itself in upheavals
and rehabilitate, sans humans.

Supposedly E.T. starships will assist Earthlings calibrate
to 5th dimensional reality if they choose it. Some folks
may request another 3D planet, return to their own planet,
another planet or accept the opportunity to 5D New Earth.
Some people will choose to die before the Shift.
The task is daunting and I wonder what I should do.

I am trying to upgrade my body and vibes.
It appears too complicated to complete all tasks
without otherworldly assistance, so I'll see what happens.
Whatever is in store for me, I'll hopefully greet it
with curiosity, creativity, commitment, unconditional love,
whether I am prepared or not--ready to go somewhere.

Maybe a Merkaba

Merkaba: divine light vehicle used by Ascended Masters to connect with and reach those in tune with higher realms. "Mer" means light. "Ka" means spirit. "Ba" means body. Considered a vehicle of ascension. Also called "chariot" in Hebrew. In Zulu—a space/time/dimension vehicle.

If Earthlings are about to be evicted
from their planet home because
we are lousy, destructive housekeepers,
so Gaia can make a clean sweep
without human house guests,
perhaps we need a get-away vehicle.

One of the steps for preparing
for a shift to 5th dimensional New Earth
calls for us to build and construct a merkaba.
A merkaba can be constructed
by male or female instructions.
It is complex--five Platonic solids
and sacred polyhedrons,
looks like pointy pyramids
and tricky triangles,
seems very hard to build.
Maybe I can order it on Amazon,
fully assembled, delivered by drone.

If matter is condensed light,
I wonder how much is involved
in creating a Light Body
for the dimensional shift, to ride in a merkaba?
If since 2012 homo sapiens
is evolving into homo luminous,
perhaps we are becoming more light-infused,
smart enough to create a merkaba
to prepare for ascension
to a peaceful, love-filled, sustainable utopia.

So while Gaia gets ready to clean house,
I need to ponder a new home elsewhere.
My next residence could be anywhere
in the cosmos, so maybe I need
to consider a merkaba for transport
or trust my soul to steer my light-spark
to my next destination—
maybe in a merkaba...
maybe not.

Ode to Homo Luminous

By shifting perception, we dream the new world into being and the world changes...a new human is emerging on Earth...homo luminous. Alberto Villoldo

Perhaps homo sapiens is due for an upgrade,
we need to evolve for the changing times.
A new light body human will cascade.
Enlightenment is what 2012 primes.
New DNA codes will repair the brain.
With new bodies we'll be whole again.

We need to evolve for the changing times
to galactic time and the feminine principle.
We will experience new paradigms.
and know dimensional lives are multiple.
Downloads will come from the sun
with new intuition for everyone.

A new light body human will cascade
from carbon to crystalline base.
Will all Earthlings make the grade
in time to enhance the human race,
before the Earth shifts to the 5th dimension
and we face death or physical ascension?

Enlightenment is what 2012 primes
into homo sapiens' awareness.
Perhaps to prepare us for new climes.
Otherworldly sources help with preparedness.
Apparently they are ready to give an uplift,
for humans to exit for the New Earth shift.

New DNA codes will repair the brain.
To create a light body which glows--
a luminous matrix manifests form and health to remain.
Where we are headed–perhaps really no one knows.
Masculine dominance in the past.
Feminine energy freed at last.

With new bodies we will be whole again.
No longer sick, thought-forms create
a peaceful realm where light will reign.
A new existence for all could indicate
a quantum leap within living generations
for self, whole planet illuminations.

Nine Codes of Light

Based on Rudolph Steiner

1. I improve my physical, mental, emotional and spiritual health.
      This aging body and mind needs constant surveillance.
      Light quality variable.   I request resilience..

2. I feel myself to be a part of the whole of life.
      I am part of a circle of life, can't know whole or pi.
      My soul's just a speck and I don't know why.

3. I know that my thoughts and feelings are as important to the world
   as my actions.
      I guess it is how I share them.
      I can't really compare them.

4. I trust that my true nature lies within.
      If I am a multidimensional being
      there may be more I'm not seeing.

5. I always follow through on my resolutions once they have been made.
      Probably not true of dark chocolate and diet,
      but can be resolute sometimes when I try it.

6. I am a being whose purpose is to give and receive love.
      Love seems to be at least this planet's goal.
      A noble purpose for any light-bearing soul.

7. I internalize only that which serves my highest well-being.
      I internalize much yearning and churning.
      Just can try my best, I'm learning.

8. I feel/express gratitude in all I receive.
      As I age, I take more time to be grateful,
      glom onto joy and dismiss the hateful.

9. I understand life as these conditions demand.
      These conditions are beyond my understanding.
      A positive uplift is what I'm commanding.

Dueling with Duality

In this yin/yang world of duality
choosing light or dark
illusion or reality
abundant or stark
       I yearn for balance not extremes–
       a place of peace, infinite dreams.

Choosing light or dark?
Light's the choice for me
unless it's dark chocolate—mark
down that I prefer not the milky.
       Light and love allow us to cope
       to face a hard life with hope.

Illusion or reality?
Probably I cannot t conceive
what is going on with certainty
with my faulty equipment to perceive.
       But I like fantasy and magic
       over what's violent and tragic.

Abundant or stark?
Conditions compound as world dims–
dire slum or lush park
often depends on human whims.
       We seem to lack self-control,
       leaving others to patrol.

I yearn for balance not extremes
as differences lead us to wars.
Earth splits at its seams
as this polluted planet's angst soars.
       Gaia's ready to shed her parasites--.
       even traffic jams other metallic satellites.

A place for peace and infinite dreams
seems a preferred cosmic plan.
A place of rainbows, sunbeams
to live in harmony, best we can.
       If we could connect positively each of us,
       we could replace joy for what's ominous.

Connecting Light

I watch light play on leaves
sun-glistens or shadows
the way light weaves,
as the wind allows
Energy loops earth to sky
continuous circle of light supply

Sun-glistens or shadows
like leaves we experience change,
each of us light-follows
as our patterns rearrange.
Sometimes we see more clearly
what we hold so dearly.

The way light weaves
head to toe through us
sews light, retrieves
what makes life wondrous.
The warp and weft on light-loom
creates a matrix so life can bloom.

As the wind allows
leaves to move,
ground fallows.
We can happily dance and love,
plug-in our reserves of sparkle
when events tend to darkle.

Energy loops earth to sky--
a never-ending cycle.
We're a needle threading brightly
letting light recycle.
From this we can infer
we are part of light transfer.

Continuous circle of light supply,
we can link to, join light flow.
We can remove blockages and try
to keep the circuit connected to glow
into enhancing healing
and playful, joyous feeling.

Into the Dark Bring Light

In the right light, at the right time, everything is extraordinary. Aaron Rose

We are starseeds sent by starlight
to bloom, glisten in earthly sunlight
nod to rest and dream in moonlight
to grow and become in daylight
wait for consciousness to alight
to ground us before flight

Each life creates its own limelight to spotlight
selects lighting–what to backlight
where to put intense floodlights
where to position phosphorescent uplight.
When choosing what to highlight,
we ponder what is mislight, lowlight, gaslight.

We see clearer with rushlight, candlelight,
torchlight flames and camp-firelight.
Bulbs, screens, mirrors exude light.
We peer at world through skylight, window-light,
follow paths by taillights and headlights,
lanterns to welcoming lighthouse or houselight.

We illuminate by lamplight,
walk through darkness with penlight, flashlight,
work on projects by droplight,
invent, collide particles by laser-light,
patrol by light meters, traffic lights.
pierce twilight by streetlight or searchlight

We dance and play when light-footed.
We laugh and love when light-hearted.
We conceive of superlight, ultralight, feather-light.
When we type, make bold a light-face.
When we lighten up we enlighten
hope we act and move lightly.

Like a diode emitting light
we are lighteners of joy to delight
share lightful knowledge to enlight.
Pay attention to lightweights and lightships,
while we experience enlightenment in earthlight.
The way to afterlife is by a tunnel of light.

From the Source of light, we inlight
express soul-light through aura-light
light-headed we seek lightening, lightsomely.

I will love the light for it shows me the way. Yet I will endure the darkness for it shows me the stars. Og Mandino

Kindle Light

In the light you will find your truth and finally you will know the power with you. Lisa Shapiro

If we can kindle light
amid darkness from within,
carry a lit candle in the night;
in darkest times like cherubim,
> we could ignite our unique spark,
> be a light presence in the dark.

Amid darkness, from within
we could draw the essence to manifest
light to let love and hope win.
Expanding light by doing our best
> can reduce negativity and darkness,
> illuminate a path away from starkness.

Carry a lit candle in the night
for soul, situation, ritual.
We can increase our insight,
help us be more spiritual.
> Enkindle a flickering flame
> to brighten the Earth game.

In darkest times like cherubim
try to wing-it, be a light source.
We don't need to be seraphim
to be a needed light resource.
> Respond to darkness in a light-ful way.
> Discern how we can assist or sway.

We could ignite our unique spark
to shine on anything that darkles.
Start with a compassionate remark,
a kind deed, smile that sparkles.
> I hope we all can get the gist
> so I can remain an optimist.

Be a light presence in the dark–
a light-bearer in all places,
enlimn pages, bloom a park,
be grateful for any graces.
> In a heavy world–uplift,
> enlighten, aid the light shift.

Acknowledgments

Other Poetry Books by Linda Varsell Smith

Cinqueries: A Cluster of Cinquos and Lanternes
Fibs and Other Truths
Black Stars on a White Sky
Poems That Count
Poems That Count Too
Winging-It: New and Selected Poems
Red Cape Capers: Playful Backyard Meditations
Star Stuff: A Soul-Splinter Experiences the Cosmos

Chapbooks

Being Cosmic
Intra-Space Chronicles
Light-Headed

On-Lone Web-site Books:
Free access @ www.rainbowcommunications.org
Syllables of Velvet
Word-Playful
Poetluck

Anthologies

The Second Genesis
Branches
Poetic License
Poetic License 2015

Some Poems in Light-Headed
from Winging-It, Being Cosmic, Light-Headed and Poetic
License 2015